Surviving Life

HOW TO TURN NIGHTMARES INTO DREAMS

Shandy Lee Loberg

Surviving Life: How to Turn Nightmares into Dreams
Shandy Lee Loberg

1. Title   2. Author   3. Memoir / Motivational / Self-Help

Library of Congress Control Number: 2014922470

ISBN 13: 9780692354063

All honor and praise go to my God in heaven for his strong, loving arms and the gracious second chance at life with which he has blessed me.

Immeasurable gratitude also goes to my mother, my husband, and my dear friend, Drew. They survived with me, cried with me, held my hand when I needed someone to hold it, and pushed me to keep going when I needed strength. You three have been my angels through this whole process, and I thank you from the bottom of my heart.

I want to thank all the people who prayed for me, shared thoughts with me, helped me with the writing process, gave financially, and supported me through this process. You all have been a blessing, for which I am thankful.

Lastly I would like to thank Lynn Varn for taking such beautiful pictures and capturing my precious family memories over the years.

TABLE OF CONTENTS

November 29, 2012

I didn't wake up that morning planning to kill myself. Actually it was just the opposite; I was feeling better than I had in a long time. Surprising, considering that just one day earlier I had been facedown in a ditch, convulsing and sobbing in pain. I had decided, just a few days shy of the anniversary of my father's death, to go finally to the rest stop where the tractor trailer he had been driving plowed into another truck and burst into flames. For ten years I had avoided this place, often taking circuitous and highly inconvenient routes to do so. Going there and really feeling the pain had given me a sense of peace I hadn't thought possible. So if someone had told me that by the next night, I would find myself revving the engine of my SUV, ready to plow into the concrete construction barrier, I would have said they were nuts. Well, I guess the saying is true—you never know where the day will take you.

The day began normally enough—breakfast with my husband Jason, getting the three older kids off to school, and strapping our youngest into the stroller for a morning jog. Then it was back to the home office to tackle my ever-growing to-do list. I was only halfway through my e-mails when the phone rang. I was tempted to let it ring, but then I saw it was Paula, one of my oldest and dearest friends.

"Hey, stranger!" she boomed, managing in those two words to convey happiness that I had answered and annoyance that I had not called her in several days.

"Sorry I've been out of touch. It's been crazy around here, with work and the kids…."

"I know. It's hard being Superwoman." Paula laughed. "But everyone needs a break. How about drinks tonight?"

I stared at the computer screen again, thought of the pile of work I had to do. What the heck? Jason can give the kids dinner, and Superwoman could use a beer.

"Sure. See you at seven."

When I arrived at the bar, Paula was already there, laying claim to a high-top table near the dartboard. When she saw me, she stood up, beer in one hand and waving with the other. She hugged me and gestured to the other side of the table, where a chair and a sweaty Miller Lite were waiting for me.

"You look great, Shandy," she said, sounding a bit surprised. She knew Dad's anniversary was approaching and probably expected me to be a mess. "You look happy."

I smiled and took a sip of my beer. "I am happy, and I'll tell you all about it after a round of darts."

Paula is older than I am, and over the years I had come to see her as a second mother—the kind you can confide in without the self-flagellation afterward. She did have the stern tone down pat, though. "No, you'll tell me now."

"I did it, Paula," I said, placing a hand on her arm. "I finally went to the rest stop."

She looked confused at first, then I saw her make the connection. "You mean—?"

"Yes."

Paula listened, her expression giving away nothing as I told how, with the support of my friend, Mark, I had finally worked up the courage to go; how I'd been shaking when I'd pulled up to the spot where my father's tractor trailer had slammed into the other truck, killing him instantly in a fiery blaze and how, even as I'd stepped out of the car and fallen sobbing to my knees, I'd known I was doing the right thing. I was purging ten years of agony.

"And that's why I'm happy." I kept an eye on Paula as I took a sip of my beer, waiting for the congratulatory hug, for her to say how proud she was of me. She had been around when my father died, and if anyone could appreciate what it took for me to go there, it was her.

Instead she flagged down the waitress for another beer and changed the subject. Surprised and rather hurt, I made halfhearted contributions to the conversation until we left the bar. I offered to give her a ride home, and with a nod she climbed into the passenger side of the SUV. We were almost to her house when I finally asked, "Don't you have anything to say about what I told you?"

Paula paused for a minute, as if debating whether to say anything. When she did answer, she sounded cold and judgmental.

"Are you crazy, Shandy? Why would you go there?"

I was so taken aback, I couldn't answer right away. I think I was waiting for her to clarify what she had said. She didn't.

"I went there to get closure."

Closure. Even to me the word now sounded like a hollow cliché, silly. I pulled the SUV into her driveway, put it in park, and turned to face her.

"Closure?" she asked. "What does that even mean? Shandy, this isn't about closure, this is about your need to create drama. All you did by going there was relive ancient history."

"I needed to feel that my father loved me, that he's forgiven me. I just need to know he is proud of me."

Paula seemed to get very irritated by the mere fact that I thought my Dad wasn't proud of me. She yelled, "Now you stop that, you stop that right now. You know your father loved you! But digging up the past is never going to help you." She leaned in closer, almost as if she was going to slap me. "Now you stop it right now, do you hear me?"

Then, ignoring my look of shock, she curtly gave me a hug, said, "Good night, love you," and got out of the vehicle. For a minute or two I sat there, watching her move toward the house and get swallowed up by the screen door. It was as if she had thrown a match into a puddle of gasoline and then walked away without a backward glance.

The eight-mile drive home was more than enough time for the poisonous thoughts to start suffocating my mind. I had been avoiding my father's death since day one, and I'd thought that going to the spot where he had died would somehow help me heal. I'd known it wouldn't make up for the fact that I'd never told him the secret I'd been carrying around since high school or that I didn't know whether he could love me after he knew what I was capable of. But I truthfully felt this was the first step in the healing process I so desperately needed. Mark had convinced me that I needed to feel the pain in order to get rid of the pain.

I turned down the dark road that led to my neighborhood, trying unsuccessfully to calm my thoughts. If Paula was right, it had been pointless to go to the rest stop. There would be no healing, no closure with my father; there would be no forgiveness. I would never get the chance to tell him the truth and hear that he loved me no matter what. I would be broken forever.

I was out of answers, out of ideas to try to make myself whole. There is no hope. The thought took root in my mind, growing larger and larger until I couldn't see past it. What most people don't understand is that suicide is not simply just an action; it is a place. The fact that this place is in our mind is irrelevant—it's still as real and palpable as our physical world. The ticket to this place is extreme pain, self-loathing, and, worst of all, an overwhelming sense of powerlessness. It is the sense that there is no earthly cure for our anguish, and the only choice left is to leave. We don't arrive at this conclusion easily, but the moment we do, nothing else exists—not our children or spouses, not our jobs or our friends. There is only the plain, blinding, and all-encompassing answer. For me, it was also a way to heaven; if I could not deal with my father's death, then I could at least join him there and finally get his forgiveness and love. I cannot even imagine the agony of those who consider suicide and do not believe in an afterlife, for they are willing to obliterate themselves entirely.

Just a few blocks from my house, I noticed the concrete barrier, and that was when my stream of consciousness began to congeal into a plan. I pulled over to the side of the road and sat there for a moment, just staring at the barrier. Then I carefully placed my left foot on the brake and shifted my right foot to the gas. I was tentative at first, listening to the roar of the engine and then letting up a few times before finally committing. I pressed the gas pedal to the floor, revving the engine until the tires were squealing and smoking, I unsnapped my seatbelt. Finally I pulled my foot from the break, and the van took off like a rocket, headed straight for the wall of concrete. I pressed my foot even harder to the gas and closed my eyes. Soon this will all be over....

I had gone a mile before I realized I was still alive and going ninety-five miles an hour. Since there were no other barriers around to crash into, I figured I might as well slow down and applied pressure to the brake. For the moment, at least, my anguish had been replaced by a vague curiosity. How was I still here? Had I chickened out at the last minute, moving the steering wheel some infinitesimal degree, just enough to miss the barrier? Was there some glimmer of hope, somewhere deep inside, that there was another way to heal my life? Or was it God letting me know I had so much more to do here? I had no idea why; all I knew was that the impulse was gone.

My body was still shaking when I pulled into my driveway and rolled the vehicle to a stop. The lights were on downstairs, and I could envision my husband, Jason, efficiently moving around the kitchen as he cleared the table or took out the trash, with no idea he had very nearly become a widower and single father of four. That was when the sobs came, convulsing my body as if I were possessed. And in a way I was, by the demons I had thought I had conquered or at least beaten into submission. I was no closer to finding the answers than I had been ten years earlier, although I had eliminated one very final one.

An hour later I pried my fingers, stiff and white-knuckled, from the steering wheel, turned off the ignition, and went inside. I can only imagine what Jason thought when he saw me—pale as a ghost, eyes nearly swollen shut from crying, flexing my right leg to loosen the sore calf muscle. He followed me to our room and watched me crawl into bed.

"Shandy? What's wrong?"

I was almost numb as I began telling him what had just happened—what I had almost done not just to myself but to him and the children. I still didn't know why I had survived, but I had to believe I had a purpose for being here, that there was a way I could heal myself and stay with my husband and children. Jason's reaction seemed to confirm this: he said nothing but looked at me with the utmost care and compassion. That night was a turning point for me simply because it had to be.

As I spoke I realized why Paula's words had sent me

into such a state. While insensitive and cruel, she had been right about one thing: going to the scene of the accident wasn't going to solve anything. I had simply built it up into an arbitrary milestone. The anniversary of my father's death, while certainly painful, was symbolic of the larger issue—my fear that people, even my own father, would reject me if they knew who I really was. The me that I had hidden from the world for so many, many years. That fear was what had led me nearly to end it all on that dark lonely road.

Over the past twenty years, I had managed to compartmentalize my life completely, locking away anything that did not fit who I was supposed to be. My rape in high school was at the top of that list. As a good Christian girl, I blamed myself for putting myself in a situation where such a thing could happen. I felt dirty and unlovable. The only thing worse than the attack itself was the fear others would find out about it, so I buried my shame and set about becoming perfect. If everyone else saw me that way, hopefully I would come to believe it as well. I had built a successful career as a public speaker, married a wonderful man, and had four beautiful children, but underneath the façade was the fear and pain, just waiting to surface.

I am not alone in this. Everyone has a survivor story. Some are more benign than mine, and others are much, much worse. It is the human condition to experience pain; it's how we deal with that pain that determines the courses of our lives. The problem is that far too many of us choose not to share our pain. We bottle it up, fearing we will be rejected, ostracized, alone. We don't realize that by not taking people into our confidence, we are forfeiting one of God's greatest gifts to us: the experience of being loved unconditionally. This is part of the reason I am writing this book. If sharing my story will help others gain freedom from past hurts and traumas; if I can help one victim of rape, one child who self-mutilates, or one person who has considered taking his or her own life, my mission has been accomplished. We cannot control everything that happens to us, but we can control how these events affect our lives.

The million-dollar question is: how do we do this? While I don't proclaim to have the answer for everyone, I can offer advice on where to begin: the Five Fs. They have helped me heal from my traumas, prioritize my goals, and live each day from a place of gratitude for what I already have.

- **Faith.** In order to turn our nightmares into dreams, we must have a belief in something greater than ourselves. This includes faith in God, of course, but it is also faith in other people as well as faith that, despite all the pain in our lives, we are here for a reason.
- **Forgiveness.** This is a highly misunderstood concept. Many people hang on to their hurt

and anger because they believe that to forgive is to let others or ourselves off the hook; however, this is not the case. Forgiveness means letting go of the behavior, releasing the pain around it, and deciding it no longer has power over your life.

- **Foundation.** These are things that keep us centered and grounded even during the most challenging times in our lives. The most important parts of our foundations are our families—those people who come into our lives not only through birth and blood but through fate. They are the people we take into our inner circles whether for life or for just a short season. When we feel like the world is against us, our families take us in, nurture us, and love us unconditionally. They love us when we are unable to love ourselves.

- **Fun.** This is something many of us overlook, especially when we are going through difficult times or don't feel deserving of enjoyment. But fun is necessary if we want to let go of painful memories and create new, joyous ones.

- **Forever.** This is best illustrated through the story I told earlier. Part of the reason Paula's words threw me into such a tailspin is that I believed my work ended with the trip to the scene of my father's accident. In reality, it had only just begun. It had only purged one layer of the pain I had been bottling up all those years. We work so hard to deal with our pain and move past it that when we make a break-through, we feel we are cured—then, when something happens to trigger our pain again, we feel even worse than before because now we feel like we are doing it wrong. We blame ourselves for not trying hard enough or not praying hard enough. Not true. It takes time, commitment, and love of self to overcome traumatic events.

As I mentioned above, the Five Fs are an excellent starting point; they are the positive things that will keep us anchored as we do the work. We must also deal with the obstacles to our healing, the biggest of which is fear. All people, even the most well-adjusted among us, have fears. The difference is that healthy people know they must conquer these fears in order to grow spiritually and have successful relationships. Throughout the book, I will discuss how I faced my greatest fear—that I would not be loved if anyone knew the real me—and how the conquering of this fear completely changed my life.

Finally it is imperative always to speak our truths. Notice I did not say the truth because let's face it: who even knows what that is? Five different people can witness an incident and give five different accounts of the so-called truth. Telling your truth is not about recounting facts as you see them; it means letting people see who you really are and what is important to you.

My mission is not entirely altruistic, however. I am writing this book as another step in my own healing. I don't believe in dishing out advice I don't follow myself, and in telling my truth I am doing just that. But most important, I am writing this book so others will realize they are not alone. Although I personally believe that with God we are never alone, it still feels that way at times, when we are wrestling with demons alone in the dark. I understand that not everyone has that belief. I have been angry with God and questioned my faith. I also have spent most of my life unable or unwilling to confide in others, so I certainly understand that. If this is where you are in your life, know that at least one other person has been there too.

Me.

CHAPTER 1

Faith

In the introduction, I mentioned how I have used the Five Fs to turn my nightmares into dreams. While all five are important, I always begin with a discussion of faith, since it serves as the foundation for everything else. Without faith, the world would be a pretty bleak place. Tragedies happen to us personally and on a global scale, and if we do not believe the situation will get better, it probably won't. Even during the worst of times, humankind has been able to pluck itself from the depths of despair, to rebound from world wars, natural disasters, and economic catastrophes. Even procreating is an act of faith, for it demonstrates our belief that the world will be here and in good enough shape to sustain our children.

Faith Comes in Many Forms

The word *faith* has come to have all sorts of implications; in recent years it has even become politically charged. People have different ideas about what it means to have faith, which has sometimes led to a rather narrow definition, followed by the exclusion of those who don't believe the same way as the larger group. That's why I want to be perfectly clear on how I define faith, the role it has played in my life, and the role it can play in yours regardless of the form it takes.

First, faith is not necessarily synonymous with religion. I have met religious people who demonstrate little faith in their daily lives, and I have met people who rarely, if ever, set foot inside a church yet have much more than the required mustard seed. Some believe faith is defined as a faith in God; some believe it means having faith in other people to love us no matter what, and still others believe it means having faith in ourselves to get the job done. My definition of faith comes back to God, who places people and situations in our lives that give us opportunities to grow spiritually and thus further us along our paths. Some are our friends and family who support and love us; others may inflict pain upon us or treat us unfairly. Friend or foe, every person we interact with is our teacher, providing us with some kernel of knowledge to be gained from having known him or her; at least that's what we believe when we have faith.

Faith Is a Choice

The first thing we must realize about faith is that it is not an emotion but a decision we make every day. Like everything else worth having, it must be continuously cultivated and nourished. When things are going well in our lives, it's easy to say we have faith. We are healthy; our bills are paid; perhaps we have found the one and are in a great relationship. But what happens during our lowest moments—when we get that terrible diagnosis from the doctor, we lose our job during corporate downsizing, or we find out our beloved spouse has been having an affair with a colleague?

When we are so angry and afraid, having even an ounce of faith seems impossible. These are the times when we must tap in to our foundation of faith. It's when our negative emotions are riding roughshod over us that we must make the conscious decision to stay strong and believe that everything that is happening has a purpose (although we may not be able to see it), and that purpose is all about our growth in our journey of faith (even if it seems like our ruination).

Everyone has heard the phrase "take it one day at a time," so much so that we consider it a cliché. Those battling substance abuse know it is a reminder to stay in the moment and have enough faith that they will make it to the next. In the beginning of their sobriety, or when times get particularly rough, they may even have to take it one hour or even one minute at a time. Faith is the same way. We have to train our minds to silence the negative chatter and focus on the good things God has already given us. Who has not felt overwhelming fear wash over them, tightening the stomach and gripping the mind? It is then that we must be able to take a step back, take a deep breath, and summon the courage to say, "No! I have faith that God will take care of me!"

In doing so we are admitting we are not in control of every circumstance and situation; we are also giving ourselves permission not to worry about these things. Instead we are giving it over to something bigger than ourselves and trusting it will be resolved for our spiritual benefit. In its simplest terms, faith means placing absolute trust in God. This kind of trust is easier to talk about than do—how many people do you know who say they trust in God and then always expect a negative outcome? This is a very painful way to live. If, on the other hand, you believe there is a plan for each of us, and that this plan is all about bringing us closer to success, to God, and to happiness, you will begin to refocus your energies on things you *can* control.

I've had to make this decision many times in my life, but one of the most difficult was after my husband and I moved our four children from O'Neill—the small town where we had built our life and laid our family roots—to Omaha. This move was very painful for me and took me to the limits of my faith and beyond. For one, I hated to leave my house. Jason and I had purchased a fixer-upper, and since he was always working, the renovations fell largely to me. I had no complaints about that; in fact I was thrilled to have the opportunity. It was almost as good as building our family's home from the ground up. But the best part was that my father helped me. We spent countless hours painting the walls, refinishing the floors, and repairing leaks, making sure every inch was perfect.

As we watched our home transform before our eyes, I could envision all the happy times we would have raising our children there. I imagined them hitting their first homers in our back yard. As teenagers, fighting over the TV remote in the living room and crowding into the kitchen after school, looking for some sugary snacks that would spoil their dinner. I thought of all the Christmases we would spend there, gathering around the tree to tear into piles of presents. My parents, who lived a mere hour away, were always part of the dream; they would be there for every holiday, every milestone in my kids' lives.

To me that house had come to represent my relationship with my father. Renovating it gave us the chance to bond in a way we never had before, and it was my way of getting the attention I had desperately craved from him as a child. After he was killed, it became a way for me to hold on to him. Every time I touched a piece of wood he had sanded or a tile he had laid, I felt like a part of him was still there with me. Now, as we packed up our things and prepared to turn over the keys to another family, I felt like I was losing him all over again.

There was also my fear of Omaha itself. As of the 2010 census, O'Neill had a population of 3,705 people. Almost everyone knew each other, and there was very little crime. Omaha, with nearly half a million people, is the largest city in Nebraska, and it seemed like every time I picked up a paper or watched the local news, there had been another carjacking, robbery, or kidnapping. Just the thought of living there scared me half to death, let alone the prospect of raising my children there. I felt like everything—my house, my sense of security, my past, my sanctuary—was being ripped away from me.

My struggle with the move led me to question everything about my life, including my marriage. For months after we arrived in Omaha, it seemed like a colossal mistake for our family in every aspect: financially, physically, and socially. Each day I tried to push back the tears and put on a brave face, but the truth of the matter was the strength of my bond with Jason was being tested in ways for which neither of us was ready.

We had gone to Omaha because Jason had always had a love for it. I believe strongly that a marriage requires equal give and take, so I had agreed to go. Although I realized it had the potential to improve our lives, I could not help but resent it. It seemed like I was following not God's will but my husband's, and that path seemed to lead us to what felt like hell on Earth to me. At one exceptionally low point, I turned to my childhood friend, Drew. We had been close for several years, and he always had a no-nonsense way of giving me advice that seemed to ring in a truer tone than the rest of the world in my ears. I knew he would tell me the truth rather than simply spout off what he thought I wanted to hear.

"Do you think God would ever take us down a path to ruin us?" I asked him after venting about my situation. It was all I had been able to think about, and while I couldn't bear the thought that God would do this, it was worse not knowing.

"Of course not!" he replied. Then he mentioned Jeremiah 29:11 and Romans 8:28, the gist of which is that God will always take care of those who love him and have faith in him. I think I made some noncommittal noise because although I have always believed this to be true, I was tired of waiting around for the payoff.

That was when Drew said the exact words I needed to hear in that moment: "Don't lose your faith, Shandy, or you will lose your hope. Pray."

Immediately my mood shifted, and I was filled with a sense of gratitude that I had such a wonderful friend in my life. The message here is that it does not always take some grand gesture to reignite your faith. Little deeds and little words can quite literally change the course of someone's life. It also serves the person providing the kindness, for it reminds them they have a larger role to play on this Earth.

It was the simple words of another friend at another low time that made a huge impact on my life. My friend, Mark, had been helping me deal with the tenth anniversary of my father's death. For the past decade, I had swallowed my feelings (along with quite a few beers), but for some reason this year my regular avoidance practices weren't working. I just couldn't handle drinking myself into oblivion; plus, no matter how much I tried to self-medicate, it didn't seem to be working. The crippling sadness would bubble up inside, ripping me apart and making it difficult to function. There had to be another way to get through that dreadful week in November, but I sure didn't know what it was. My poor husband didn't know how to help me carry my load, and for some reason reaching out to my family only made my pain worse. I started to shut down, shutting out everything and everyone in my life so no one could see my agony.

Through tears of desperation one day, I unloaded my story to Mark.

"Let yourself feel the pain," he said simply and encouraged me to stop by the place where my father had been killed.

I was struck by a realization that maybe the simplest

solution is the best. Of course that didn't mean it was going to be easy for me to do it. "I have ten years of pain pent up. I am afraid of what could happen if I let it out. What if I can't get up after I stop?"

"Call me then," Mark replied. "I'll be there for you."

As I mentioned in the introduction, I would stop there, and I did feel an enormous sense of release of the pain I had been carrying around for so long. And despite Paula's rather callous attitude about my breakthrough and all that came after, I have never regretted going there. Some people, like Mark and Drew, make us feel loved and supported; others, like Paula, make us feel stupid and alone. The trick is to understand (and have faith) that they are all teachers, motivators, and catalysts for healing.

Faith Evolves over Time

Faith is a living, breathing thing; as we learn and grow, so does our definition of faith. As I said earlier, this may be at odds with our family, friends, and community who think differently than we do. However if we want to build a foundation of faith, we must first discern what it means for us personally.

I had a strict religious upbringing. My church's definition of faith as I saw it was built on strict obedience to its rules. Some of these rules were pretty standard for Christians—for example, remaining a virgin until marriage—while mainstream society would see others as rather extreme. For example, they frowned upon dancing.

By the time I was fourteen, my life had been mapped out for me. I was dating a young man several years older than I was. He also attended my church, and my mother, my father, and the rest of the congregation assumed we would one day marry, have children, and then raise them the same way we had been raised. Even at that young age, however, I was not convinced this was the life for me. There was the sense I did not fit, that there was something else out there for me.

Of course in that young mind-set, this was just a nagging feeling in the back of my head, and it manifested itself in the form of teenage rebellion. While I cared deeply for my boyfriend, I was in no way certain he was the person I wanted to spend the rest of my life with. In order to test the boundaries, I would call it off one week and get back together with him the next, often dating other boys during the off periods. These relationships, like the one with my boyfriend, pushed the boundaries of innocence without ever crossing the ultimate line. But it was still outside my parents' and the church's expectations. It felt great to assert my independence, but at the same time I could not help feeling I was risking God's approval.

I was certainly skating on thin ice with the congregation. After having attended a religious camp for many years, I had applied to be a counselor to the younger kids. When I received a letter from the camp council stating I was "unsuitable to shape Christian minds" because I had attended a school dance, I was completely devastated. The council members were pillars of our religious community, and I had been taught since birth to revere my elders; therefore when they said I was unacceptable, it was as if God himself were condemning me. I felt worthless and acted out in ways that were not healthy for me spiritually or physically.

It would be many years before I came to understand that the council's decision, while painful, had been another hint from God that I was not where I needed to be. My faith was going to evolve and lead me in a different direction. Today I have a broader definition of faith that has allowed me to grow as a person and still feel I am deserving of God's love, forgiveness, and blessings. I am not judging the church in which I grew up or their view of faith; I am merely acknowledging that I did not fit into it. You see, faith is first a relationship between ourselves and God. We must understand and define what it means for us before we can share with others. I will expand upon this topic further in the chapter on foundation.

Faith Has No Time Limit

Many of us think we have faith. We tell ourselves—and God—that we believe he will deliver the career we want, the perfect spouse, house, the kids, the clean bill of health. Then, when these things do not come right away (or in the exact way we want them), we become angry and disappointed. We are disillusioned not only with God but with ourselves for being naïve/foolish/wishful thinkers. Our attitude becomes even more negative than it was before we decided to go out on that limb.

But faith is something we must choose every day. There will always be something to worry or pray about, and the situation at hand will not always be resolved according to our schedules. Sometimes we do not have the answer for days, months, or even years. Herein lies the real test of faith.

Let's return for a moment to the church council that denied my application to be a camp counselor because I had danced. Although I was too young to realize it at the time, I had stepped outside my church's definition of faith and into what many spiritual people refer to as the void. It is the perfect word, too, because it describes how you feel when you have left something behind but cannot yet see where you are headed. You are in no man's land. I liken it to travelling down a pitch-black road, with only the meager light from dim headlights to guide you. You cannot see the twists and turns until you are upon them, and all you want to do is get where you're going—and fast. It's much like driving my SUV toward that concrete barrier. It wasn't that I wanted to die; it was that I was sick of not knowing how I was going to deal with the pain in my life, and I just wanted the turmoil to end once and for all. However, when we are in this terrifying place of not knowing, faith is most important. We are telling God, "I don't know how this is going to turn out or *when* it will be resolved, but I am placing my trust in you and believe you will take care of me and resolve this situation at the perfect time and for my highest good."

Oftentimes our faith is tested in order to give us chances to grow. Not long after our move to Omaha, I had to return to Western Nebraska to give a weeklong training. I was still feeling out of sorts in my new surroundings and overwhelmed by a personal and professional to-do list the likes of which even I had never seen. Still, I was in a good mood as I packed for the trip.

There was only one thing that was troubling me: in order to get to the training, I would have to drive right past my old home. As I pulled the car out of the driveway, I thanked God for the strength to face this demon. I was still thankful as I began the eight-hour drive. However, the closer I got to my old life, the more my faith began to waiver. Suddenly I was no longer sure I could face seeing the house again. I had heard that the new owners had not been taking care of it the way we had, and the mere thought of seeing it in disrepair threatened to destroy my fragile peace of mind. I would have been more than happy to avoid it altogether, but there was no other route.

As I got closer to O'Neill, my heart grew heavier until it was filled with an overwhelming sadness. Suddenly I was no longer thinking about engaging my audience at the training; instead I was thinking about all the things I had left behind in the move, like the quiet streets and the feeling of safety that comes from knowing everyone in town. It was all continuing on without me, as if I had never lived there.

When I saw the house I was so upset, I had to pull over to the side of the road. Barely able to breathe, I just sat there for a few moments before getting out of the car. The stories I'd heard were true—the new owners were not keeping up with the yardwork. The grass was wilted and brown in patches, and my flowers—some of them gifts from my grandmother—were dead. When I saw that our name was still on the mailbox, it was the final straw. I felt as if someone had desecrated my father's grave. I felt as if they were living *my* life.

My eyes were blurring with tears as I pulled my cell phone out of my pocket and began snapping a few pictures of the house and yard. Suddenly it struck me that I was not just sad; I was enraged at both Jason and God for making me give up this haven I had loved so much. I was also terrified that I would not be able to make my new living situation work. What if this anger destroyed my marriage? What if it destroyed my ability to parent my children? The last thing I wanted was to disclose my fears to them.

This brought on a mini epiphany. The only way to refrain from passing down my fear, anger, and resentment to my children was to conquer those emotions. The only way to do so was to have faith God would lead me through this challenge as he had all the others. Fighting my urge to knock on the door and chastise the new owners for letting my plants die, I got back in the car. As I drove away, my sadness was replaced by a growing sense of accomplishment. God was reminding me to be authentic and bold with my faith.

A week later, as I was driving back to Omaha, back to a life I hated, the anger against my husband once again began to rise to the surface. I realized I would soon have to conquer the second F: forgiveness.

Faith Requires a Leap

Have you ever fumbled around a dark room, searching for the light switch? You cannot see where you are going or what obstacles await you. The light switch eludes you, and finally you have to stop hugging the wall, step out into the darkness, and believe you'll find a lamp. Well, that's kind of like faith—you already have tried to find the quick fixes to your problems, but in the end you must step out into the unknown and have faith that illumination will follow.

Right now you might be saying, "Yeah, right, easy for you to say." But actually it's not. I've had to take several terrifying leaps in my life, and I expect I'll be taking several more. They never really get easier, either; each situation brings its own challenges and seems to up the ante. Here's the thing, though: no one, not even the world's greatest political leaders, innovators, and religious figures, knows what they are capable of unless they have taken a risk.

Sometimes the leap requires us to have faith in another person or, more accurately, have faith that our hopes for that relationship are in line with God's plan. Everyone who gets married has to take this kind of leap, but some—like me—have to leap a little further than others. The first time Jason and I were engaged, he and I were living together with my sister in Omaha. By that time we had been dating for several years, and I was starting to wonder whether our relationship would ever get to the next level. My mother shared my concern and had begun pressuring him to pop the question.

Being the standup and traditional person he is, Jason did ask me to marry him. I happily accepted, but as the months passed I realized he was not all that interested in the wedding planning. At first I thought he was like the millions of other guys who don't consider party planning their forte, but it was more than this. In fact he spent more time hanging out and playing PlayStation with my sister than helping me with the arrangements. Anxious and frustrated, I became unbearable to live with, constantly bossing everyone around. This was long before *Bridezillas* hit the airwaves, or I probably could have had an episode all to myself.

One day my sister and I went flower shopping for the wedding. When we came home, Jason wasn't there, and I figured he hadn't returned from the softball tournament he'd attended that morning. We had just starting making arrangements for the altar when I noticed that our puppy was carrying around a half-chewed notebook. I scrambled to take it from him, and that was when I saw the note in Jason's handwriting. I scanned the words, my mouth literally dropping open.

"What do you think of this one?" my sister asked, pointing to an especially lovely arrangement. "Shandy? What's wrong?"

I didn't answer her, just ran to the bedroom and whipped open the closet door. There, next to my crisp, white wedding gown, was a series of empty hangers. Jason's clothes were gone. He must have packed up his stuff and taken it with him when he had left for the game. As I trudged back out to the living room, I felt as though my body was weighted with lead. I sputtered out some words to my sister and then picked up the phone to call Mom. Looking back I can only imagine how angry and hurt she was. She swallowed her own feelings and tried, quite unsuccessfully, to calm me down. By that afternoon she and my father were there with a trailer to pack up my things and take me back home, where no one could hurt me.

As it turned out, Jason did not want to end our relationship completely. He still loved me, he said when he called the house and got past whichever parent had answered the phone. He just did not feel we were ready for marriage. He thought our relationship needed some work. Was I willing to do that? Still reeling from his sudden departure, I didn't know if I was willing. What if I gave him another chance only to have him leave me again? I had believed he was the right man for me, but now I wondered if it had just been wishful thinking. I knew I had to take a leap of faith in order to trust Jason again and trust God to show us the best path.

Over the next several months, Jason and I did work on our relationship, and I began to see that he had been right to postpone the wedding. During that time we both prayed on it, and Jason gave his life over to Christ. By the time our previously scheduled wedding was supposed to happen, I had my answer. Jason proposed to me again. The second time around, it was a completely different experience: we threw together a simple yet very elegant wedding in six weeks, and I had the peace of mind of knowing that Jason was as committed to the marriage as I was.

More recently Jason and I took another leap of faith when he decided to quit his job at a major retail vending company where he had worked for thirteen years. He had loved his job as a route manager for the company back in O'Neill; he had been earning a nice salary, and his hours had allowed him ample time to spend with the kids and me. So when we were making plans to move to Omaha, he didn't even apply to other companies—he just put in a transfer request, which the company quickly granted.

It wasn't long before we realized the job was the same in name only. Jason was responsible for delivering products to stores along his route. Although those stores had closed early in a tiny town like O'Neill, they were open very late—sometimes twenty-four hours a day—in Omaha. The schedule was grueling, with Jason having to get up at 3:00 a.m. and work like a dog all day only to pass out in the early evening, around the same time as the children. Even worse, the transfer had come with a rather large pay cut. I suddenly felt as though I was raising four kids by myself, and the rare times when Jason and I were together were strained.

The leap came when Jason announced he couldn't take it anymore and was leaving the company. He had found a job selling widows and siding. Knowing that our family couldn't continue this way, I agreed. And indeed, the schedule for his new job was much better; Jason was able to eat dinner with us again, and I got to speak to him without having him fall asleep midsentence.

There was only one problem: he wasn't making any money. He was trying to sell these windows door to door, and most of those doors were being slammed in his face. As we watched our bank account decreasing by the day, we began to wonder whether God had forgotten our address. Again we prayed for the strength to keep the faith that things would improve.

Rock bottom came early one morning as I was preparing to hit the road for work—three speeches in three days; forty hours of driving for three hours of work. I was just getting out of the shower when I heard Jason moaning. He was still in bed, hurting so badly his eyes rolled back in his head and tears rolling down his face. When I asked him what was wrong, he replied, "I think I am dying. Seriously, Shandy, I need to go to the hospital."

I went into crisis mode, getting my oldest up to babysit everyone without trying to cause a panic. I got Jason into the car, and within minutes we were speeding to the nearest emergency room. When the doctors told us he was passing an exceptionally large kidney stone and would be fine, I almost fell to my knees with relief. It hit me that for as stressed as we were about our finances, we were so richly blessed in other ways.

The next day, still hopped up on painkillers and worried about the lack of income his job provided, Jason informed the windows and siding company it was time for him to leave. A few hours after that, he got a job offer from another company—also in sales but a business-to-business position with excellent earning potential plus a benefit package we had severely been missing. The point of all of this? If Jason hadn't taken the leap to leave his retail vending job, our family may have experienced irreparable damage. By following what he felt called to do, he was able to spend more time with us and ultimately land a better job in the process. But the process is never easy.

Gratitude Is an Essential Component of Faith

If Jason's health scare taught us anything, it was that no matter where we are in our journey or what our present circumstances, we all have something for which to be grateful. It may be something big, like a positive report from the doctor, or it may be something small, like kindness from a stranger. When we are grateful for what we already have, we have the faith to invite more good into our lives. We understand that God is always working in our lives on several levels, even if the details are not clear to us. Some people are not there yet; others are going through a period of doubt. In either case we discover or recover our faith by looking at the positives.

Having gratitude does not mean we are ignoring reality or do not strive to accomplish more. However, it is essential to building a foundation of faith. Remember: having faith is a choice we must make every day. Looking at the positives and the blessings in each day can give us the fuel we need to make the ultimate choice of faith. If you have faith, you have hope!

Questions to Ask Yourself

1. What is your definition of faith?
2. Who has been placed in your life to help you along your path? How did they help?
3. Think about a time when you took a leap of faith. How did it turn out?
4. What did you learn from your leap?
5. How strong do you consider your faith to be? How can you improve your faith?

CHAPTER 2

Forgiveness

The concept of forgiveness has to be one of the most debated and misunderstood in history. The Bible encourages us to forgive others as God forgives us, yet even the most devout people have a difficult time with this. As we make our way through life, it is inevitable that we'll be tossed about by circumstances and wounded by the people we love. We will also hurt others, intentionally and unintentionally, due to our own human frailties. No matter who is wounded or who is doing the wounding, both parties are left feeling angry and betrayed. We can try to ignore these emotions; we can lash out at others, or we can punish ourselves. However, we will never really be able to heal until we learn how to forgive.

As a society we are conditioned to feel uncomfortable with anger. It is seen as a distasteful emotion, a sign of being out of control and sometimes a precursor to violence and cruelty. Yet anger is not always a bad thing. In fact when channeled in a positive way, it can be a powerful motivator for good. It can help us right wrongs not only in our personal lives but on a global scale. Research any great movement—whether it was to abolish apartheid in South Africa or to integrate the school systems in the American South—and you will learn it began with people who were angered by the status quo and came together to provoke change.

When anger is released in an unhealthy way, it is one of the most destructive forces in life. Think about the pain you feel when someone expresses anger with you. It doesn't matter whether they yell and scream or give us the cold shoulder. We just want to find a way to make it right. We want to return to our previous relationship prior to the hurtful words, the broken promise, or whatever caused the anger. We rarely stop to consider that the angry person is also in pain, caused by the real or imagined offense or maybe from the anger itself. Unchecked anger leaves us unsettled and puts us on edge. It robs us of our peace. Even worse, anger does not dissipate over time; instead it festers, rotting through everything in its path.

Forgiveness Is a Decision

Remember back in chapter one, when I said that Faith is a decision? Fittingly it is the same with forgiveness. When we are hurt or angry about acts perpetrated upon us, it may seem as if our feelings are anything *except* choices—we feel as if our emotions own us. This is especially true when the injustice has a lasting effect on our life. For example, a colleague sabotages our work at the office, preventing us from getting that promotion or even causing us to lose our job. It is a long journey to get back on our feet, during which time we're dealing with ongoing pain, anxiety, anger, or even financial ruin. Forgiving that person feels like we're overlooking the behavior. It feels like we are giving in to our power-lessness when in fact the opposite is true. Letting go is the key to our freedom.

On the other hand, if letting go is so great, why is it so hard to do? Could it be because it is also one of the scariest things we will ever do? We are largely a collaboration of our memories and experience, both good and bad. As children we witnessed certain things in our homes. We noticed which kids were popular at school and which ones were bullied. As teenagers we experienced broken hearts and probably broke others' hearts as well. Whether we realize it or not, our personalities changed in response to these things. We developed defense mechanisms to prevent us from being hurt again. I can honestly say that anytime I ever hear someone say the words "we need to talk," I immediately stall them. I spend the next several hours running over every possible bad scenario we can possibly have to talk about. That way I am prepared, with my walls built for anything that may come my way once we sit down. It's part of my defense mechanism. We journey through life building up this armor, thinking it will shield us from the ugliness of our existence.

Unexpectedly one day something gets past our defenses; we are blindsided by a person we trusted or a circumstance we never saw coming. Suddenly our defense mechanisms no longer work. This is exactly what happened to me the night I attempted to plow my SUV into the barrier. After years of avoiding my father's death, it required only a few insensitive words from a friend to send me over the edge. That night was a wake-up call—I had to deal with my emotions and forgiveness issues, or I might not live to see my kids grow up! For me it began with confiding in my husband when I went in the house that night, taking off my armor, and letting him see the real me and the hell existing inside my mind. It wasn't easy by any means. Next step, the most important of all, was forgiving me, which I will address later.

As much as we may want to let go of the hurt, it feels like doing so is giving up a part of ourselves, such as who we are and what we have endured. Once we make the decision to let go, we realize we have been dragging an anchor around rather than wearing a shield. It has been weighing us down, altering every decision we make. It is the whisper in our head, telling us we can't or won't because we are unworthy.

For me it was the voice telling me, "No one could love you if they really knew you." It had felt comforting and safe to live this way and believe the voice since there was no fear of the unknown. Although embracing the unknown was necessary for me and for you to move onward and upward. Remember, when you allow the past to define you, you are also allowing it to write your future. It becomes a self-fulfilling prophecy.

Forgiveness Moves Us Past Anger, Toward Gratitude

When something bad happens to us, we not only blame other people, we also blame God. We tell ourselves he has forgotten us, he has forsaken us, or He's punishing us for our sins. Sometimes we jokingly chalk it up to his sick sense of humor. Regardless of what we think God's reasoning is, we believe he has decided in his infinite wisdom we are not worthy of receiving what we want, or we are deserving of hardship and tragedy.

This core belief directly affects our self-esteem and

ability to embrace the good things in life. When we hurt we think it's our lot; when things are good we are constantly waiting for the other shoe to drop. I could spend time trying to convince you God is not a sadistic joker who enjoys watching us suffer but a loving entity who wants everyone to experience happiness and peace. However, I won't do that. I believe each person must reach those conclusions by himself or herself. Instead I am going to suggest you consider a simple shift in perspective.

I had a difficult time forgiving God after he took my father away. Dad was a truck driver, and on December 7, 2002, he was heading down I-80 for a weeklong trip. He was approaching a rest stop when, according to the state patrol's report, his truck drifted twelve inches over the white line and struck the back of another semi that was illegally parked on the side of the road. He hit that truck so hard, he pushed it into another truck, throwing that driver from his bunk where he was sleeping. My dad's truck was full of fuel and burst into flames on impact. Another truck driver came running with a fire extinguisher and tried to put out the fire, but it was already engulfing the cab. He told the police he could hear my Dad's desperate cries for help, and the awful helplessness he felt when he realized there was nothing he could do. It all ended in an explosion that threw my father's charred body from the wreckage. After conducting the autopsy, the coroner speculated that Dad might have suffered a heart attack behind the wheel, causing his truck to swerve. He was only fifty-four.

When I learned of my father's death, I fell to the floor, screaming in agony. It felt as though someone had dropped an entire brick building on my body. When I learned of the horrible circumstances, that agony turned to rage—not only at the driver that had parked illegally, but at God. How could He have let my father, a man who had always served him so faithfully, suffer that way? And how could he have done this to my mother, our family, and me? Not only had we lost Dad, but we had also been robbed of the closure of seeing him in his casket.

A respected church leader and neighbor told me shortly after, "It is okay to be upset with God, just don't ever turn your back on him because of it." Nevertheless, no matter how I tried, I continued to harbor my anger, holding it close to my heart. Why had he taken my Dad away at a time when I still needed him so much? Why did he have to make him burn the way he did, causing my last memory of him to be a cold, hard box? Why didn't I ever get the chance to tell Dad what pain I endured in high school?

The questions plagued me night and day, but there were no answers in sight. Every time I experienced a shred of sadness or longing for my father, it would instantly turn to rage. Whenever I felt it bubbling up inside me I would force it down quickly to avoid the pain it brought. It wasn't just the pain of my father's tragic death; it was the feeling of being betrayed by God, a being I had been taught to believe was all knowing, all loving, and all merciful. If there was mercy and love in having my family suffer this way, I could not see it. Even worse, I felt as though my faith was eroding. What was wrong with me that I could not accept this as part of God's plan? It would take me a long time to forgive God and to forgive myself for doubting him. I realized that my anger at him was part of my grieving process, and at some point I would have to let that anger go.

The next time you feel God has denied you something (or worse, taken away something you already had), you need to consider the bigger pictures, change your perspective a little. God sometimes takes the great people out of our lives so we can learn to be great on our own, as was the case with my father. Or possibly he has spared you from a potentially harmful person or situation that was not for your highest good. This is *not* a copout; it's not about crossing your arms and saying, "Well, I didn't want that job anyway." It is about calmly and objectively looking at the situation.

Of course in the moment, and because our human minds and eyes can see only what is in front of us, we cannot always see that it's for the best. This is where faith steps in. Remember, faith has no time limit. We have to believe things are happening for the best, even when we cannot feel that idea. We cannot rely on feelings. We must rely on belief and trust that good will become apparent even if it takes days, months, or even years. Perhaps it never will be clear to us while we are on Earth. When we begin to trust our faith, we will not only forgive God, but we can thank him in advance for taking care of us, even in our most desperate times.

Forgiveness Saves Close Relationships

There is a saying: we always hurt the ones we love. Well, the ones we love are also the hardest to forgive. They wound us more deeply than anyone else since we trusted them to safeguard our hearts. When they break that trust, it forces into question everything we believed about them, ourselves, and our lives. Consequently it is so incredibly painful to move past it. In fact it may be difficult even to process what has happened. We may be shocked; we may even feel guilty for being angry at that person (especially if it's a parent or spouse). But we must allow ourselves time to feel the pain and work through it rather than push it down. Only then can we truly begin to think of forgiving them.

If forgiveness seems impossible, you must take a step back and honestly look at the alternatives. You can end the relationship, which in most cases will be extremely painful for both of you (and never really solve the problem but compound it instead). You can pretend to forgive them, but the anger will eventually begin to erode your bond from the inside out. Or you can work through the pain and make the decision to forgive them. This will take work; you may have to take baby steps to repair the relationship or even seek the help of a counselor. Just realize that whether you choose forgiveness or not, you are making a decision that will either end the relationship or lead to a healthier, more authentic one.

More than any other close relationship, marriage demands both parties be willing to forgive each other *on a regular basis.* This makes having a happy marriage so challenging and so elusive. When two people marry, they are asking each other to accept their respective experiences, viewpoints, and personalities *for the rest of their lives.* There are no blood ties binding them, as there are with children or parents. However, there is an escape route—divorce—if things fall apart or get too difficult.

The one thing holding a couple together is the strength of their commitment. Forgiveness goes to the heart of this commitment and is implicit in the vows. Without it this unique bond will never survive the trials and daily grind, not to mention the curveballs life throws us along the way.

Forgiveness Releases Us from Toxic Situations

Anger not only drives a wedge between us and the people we love; it also binds us to the people we should let go. When we are angry with someone, we tend to spend a great deal of energy thinking and talking about them. Think of all the people who are involved in nasty divorces. Each is so obsessed with making the other suffer, they waste their own life in the process. When we hang on to anger, we replay conversations in our head and think about what we could have said to get the better of the person who hurt us. We discuss them with others, trying to purge the negativity and justify our continuing involvement in the situation. Underneath it all we wonder what we did to deserve the lousy treatment. Consequently, while we believe we do not deserve it, we are perpetuating it.

This is a sticky point for a lot of people. They confuse forgiveness with allowing someone to walk all over them. They say, "But why should I let that person get away with…?" when really the person they're keeping on the hook is themself. Forgiveness is not about letting the person off the hook, and it is not about being a pushover. If there is reasonable action you can take to resolve the situation, by all means take it. File the lawsuit, call off the wedding, or give him or her a piece of your mind. Just know once you have done and said everything you can, it is time to let it go.

What if someone has done something truly appalling? Is he or she really deserving of forgiveness, and how do you make the decision? This point of forgiveness is something reasonable minds can and have disagreed on since the beginning of time. Some believe worthiness depends on one's desire to redeem himself or herself. Catholics go to confession with the intent of unburdening their sins to a priest; they believe if they are truly repentant, God will forgive them. Others believe whether one should be forgiven depends upon the seriousness of the harm done—for example, someone who steals because he is in desperate need of the money versus someone who preys on children. A victim may be able to forgive the former but will likely spend a lifetime trying to forgive the latter. Should you forgive someone who shoves you down, wraps their hands around your neck, and steals your innocence? That is a question for philosophers and theologians. God says yes, forgive as he has forgiven.

The fundamental truth is that forgiveness is necessary for you to move on. Whether the guilty party is *ultimately* forgiven is between him or her and God. That being said, it is a wonderful and empowering feeling to grant forgiveness to a person who is truly sorry for what they've done. However, what about the person who expresses no regrets? Remember: while forgiveness is sometimes about freeing the other person, it is *always* about freeing yourself. You can forgive the action, however only God can forgive the heart.

Forgiveness Is Ongoing

Some things are relatively easy to forgive. Let's say, for example, you have a friend or colleague with whom you've always gotten along. Then one day you have an argument with this person. Things get blown out of proportion. You both say hurtful things, and you storm out. After you've had time to cool down, you look at the totality of your relationship and decide it's not worth ending things. So you forgive them, hope they forgive you, and move on. In time you may even find the argument, as terrible as it was, was actually a good thing—it cleared the air and strengthened the friendship.

Other things, however, require ongoing forgiveness. Perhaps it was an offense so atrocious, it wounded you to the core. Perhaps it is an ongoing behavior that has continued far too long. Whatever the case, you may find you have forgiven the person one day only to awaken angry the next. You keep replaying the situation in your mind, wondering why they did this to you and what you could have done to avoid or put a stop to it.

Back in chapter one, I talked about how devastated I was when my family moved from O'Neill to Omaha.

I was also very angry I had to leave the home and the community I loved for a place I considered a cold and possibly dangerous city. This anger was largely directed at my husband, Jason. He had loved living in Omaha previously and had always dreamed of moving back. Still, when he seriously broached the subject of a transfer, I fought it tooth and nail. The thought of leaving our home and ripping our children from the safety of a small town was appalling to me.

On the other hand, I felt I had to consider it. Jason had always supported my personal dreams and goals; hence it was only fair I support his dreams as well. I stated my case for staying. Nevertheless, in the end I gave in. Maybe it was, as Jason said, God's will that we made this change. However, once we were there, in a new place, financially strapped and without friends, I began to believe it had little to do with God's will and everything to do with my husband's will!

Each day I found something else to hate about Omaha and something more to miss about my old life; each day I resented Jason just a little bit more. Despite being married with four children, I felt alone and powerless over my own life. I felt like Jason had put me in a prison. As time went on, the resentment grew; there were even days when I considered taking the kids and escaping to a place where he would never find us.

Frightened by my own anger and despair, I knew if I did not find a way to deal with this resentment, it was going to ruin our marriage. I *had* to forgive Jason for uprooting our family.

As soon as I made the decision, I felt not only immense relief but a sense of empowerment. I was going to do something that would make everything better. However, it wasn't long before the anger began to well up again because I spent more evenings alone, as Jason went to sleep as soon as the kids did. To add insult to injury, I watched the money dwindling in our bank account because he had taken a pay cut.

Then one night I saw yet another disturbing news story—an attempted kidnapping had occurred not far from our home. I completely freaked out. I'd never worried about these things in O'Neill! In an instant I was back in escape mode; I even texted my mother that I was considering leaving. That was when a new insight popped into my mind. I realized some problems require constant forgiveness. I would not get over my anger toward Jason all at once. I would have to make a choice each day to forgive him, even as I was dealing with the consequences of the move. This leads me to my next point, which is recognizing our own role in causing and perpetuating our pain and our power to eradicate it.

Forgiveness Means Taking Responsibility

Oftentimes we are so caught up in what someone else has done to us, we cannot see our own role in perpetuating the pain. While I had every right to hate life in Omaha, it wasn't fair of me to place all the blame on my husband. He was not some dictator, ordering me to go. We'd had several discussions in which he'd stated his case for moving, and I had stated mine for staying in O'Neill. Eventually I had decided—albeit against my better judgment—to give Omaha a try. I was aware of the risks of his making less money and of the enormous adjustments I would have to make. However, I chose to have faith in my husband and in God that this was the right path for our family.

Right now you might be thinking, *Okay,* you *played a part in* your *outcome;* you *agreed to the move. But I played no part in my spouse's leaving me or my friend's deceiving me, my firm's downsizing me, etc.!*" What you must realize is there is a difference between being at fault and taking ownership of the problem. For example, perhaps you have known for some time you and your spouse were not as close as you used to be. However, rather than sitting down and inviting him or her to communicate, you avoided the situation, blaming it on kids, busy schedules, etc. You made excuses like, "This happens to every marriage after a while." Or perhaps everything seems fine on the surface, but you've noticed your spouse is suddenly working late every night or walks out of the room to answer phone calls. Instead of asking him or her what's going on, you bury your head in the sand only to be shocked when the infidelity is revealed. Shock turns to rage. Over time the rage will eat you up inside, making it impossible to heal.

These examples may seem harsh, which is precisely why I am using them to illustrate this point. If we say we're ready to transform our nightmares into dreams, we must be willing to deal with the worst of them. Holding on to anger keeps us powerless against not only the hurtful person or situation but also our own emotions. We are all the stars of our own dramas, and the only way we can get power back is to take ownership of our realities and our roles in creating them.

Sometimes the opportunity to step up comes only *after* the painful event has occurred; such as when we are blindsided by an illness, an accident, or the loss of a job. It is only human to pity ourselves and rage at the world. In fact it is a necessary part of the healing process and far preferable to burying our feelings. Sooner rather than later, you will have to let go of that rage and accept the fact that you and only you are responsible for making the most out of your circumstances.

As you know by now, I did not write this book because I think I've always handled my problems the right way—quite the opposite. For years I engaged in terribly destructive behaviors for the sole purpose of burying my pain. Hard times are inevitable; it is impossible to avoid them no matter who we are. What is ultimately important is that we deal with them in healthy ways; otherwise they can literally be the death of us.

For reasons I still don't understand, I began avoiding my feelings—particularly negative emotions—at a pretty young age. When something bothered me, I shoved it down so deep, I could almost convince myself I had no pain or at least that it didn't affect me in any real way. The way I saw it, feelings were uncontrollable and undependable, therefore dangerous. I thought I was being strong by avoiding them.

By the time I was a teenager, I was dealing with unpleasant life events in a very extreme physically harming fashion. I would cut myself with a razor blade. Not deep; nothing that would require stitches but drawing blood just the same. The first time was in the eighth grade, right after Tim and I had one of our many breakups. I have no memory of what gave me the idea or why I was suddenly compelled to take the sharp sliver of metal, bring it to my skin, and begin slicing. I just know when I first felt the burning sensation of the blade and winced as it cut through my skin, I felt relief. I saw the thin stream of blood, but I did not stop. I just moved the blade half an inch over and did it again. I was hooked. To me dealing with physical pain was infinitely easier than dealing with uncomfortable emotions.

I was well aware this behavior was strange, maybe even crazy, so I tried whatever I could do to cover up the cuts. Back then no one had ever heard of cutters except those who actually did it and, if they were lucky enough to get help, their shrinks. We now know it is a very dysfunctional, very common attempt to cope with rage, pain, and loneliness. Like me, most cutters are girls in early adolescence who, for whatever reason, would rather hurt themselves than confide in parents, friends, and teachers.

Looking back I think I may have done it because I did not want my mother and father to know I didn't fit their expectations. They assumed I would eventually marry Tim, have children, and raise them in the same town where I had grown up; I was not at all sure I wanted these things. Of course I desired a husband and a family, but I also wanted to go to college, have a career, and see places outside my small, insular world. And unlike my parents, I was not convinced I should spend the rest of my life with Tim. Disappointing my parents—especially my father—was simply not an option for me, so I took the razor to myself.

As I made those thin slices against my flesh, it was as if all the feelings of powerlessness and loneliness were being released out of me and into the droplets of blood.

It was the only time I felt any sense of peace. It also gave me a sense of control—there was no emotion I could not control when I was cutting! Whenever something bothered me, I would just push it to the back of my mind and then slip into my bedroom as soon as I got the chance. Problem solved, and no one had to know. Now that I am a parent, I know with complete certainty that my parents would have chosen disappointment in their daughter's choices than to have a daughter who self-mutilated.

Where had I learned the idea that negative feelings were to be concealed like a dirty secret? Was I born that way, or was there some subtle dynamic in my family that convinced me it was better to bury my emotions? I don't know. Years later, after my father passed away, my mom told me, "It's OK to cry and be sad, Shandy." What she didn't know was that by the time I was twenty-eight, I was completely disconnected from my emotions. To add insult to injury, I also felt as though I had never truly been a child even though my parents had always made sure I had a good childhood. I had been safe, clothed, fed, cared for, and loved. Despite all of that, I always thought of myself as the adult, trying to keep it together so I could take care of my family. When my parents fought, I thought I was responsible for fixing it. I also believed I had to take care of my brother and sister. I even recall trying to figure out how to start my own business and raise money, so my parents wouldn't have financial problems anymore. And this was all before middle school!

I have no idea why I took on so many adult burdens as a child or why it took me so long to love myself, but it does not matter. I cannot change the past, and I truly believe that things happened the way they were meant to in order to teach me certain lessons. One thing I have learned is my time is better spent owning and being responsible for my journey than wishing I could change it.

Forgiving Yourself Sets Your Heart Free

I've known for a long time how important it is to forgive those who have hurt us; I also knew that in order to move forward spiritually we must forgive God. However, it took me almost ending my own life on that dark road before I realized the person I needed to forgive most was myself. It was the self-hatred I had been carrying around for twenty years, since the night I was raped, that was causing me so much anguish.

It happened during my senior year of high school. By that time I had been dating Tim since I was thirteen. As I said before, my life had been planned out for me, but I wasn't sold on this plan. Over the years I had flirted with rebellion, mostly by breaking up with Tim. It was my way of asserting the small amount of control I had and perhaps trying on other directions I might take in life. I would hang out with my friends and go on dates with other boys, but after a while I'd always return to the safety of my relationship with Tim and the approval of my parents.

It was during one of these off periods that I met the man who would attack me. He didn't live in town but was part of a six-man crew that travelled from place to place, painting barns for farmers. In a community of about seven hundred people, these guys were big news, especially among the teenage girls. They were cute, a couple of years older than us, and had an air of mystery about them. My friends and I had crushes on them in general, but there was one in particular—I'll call him Joe—who caught my eye. Joe was friendly, handsome, and drove a new teal Corvette convertible that for me signified freedom and extravagance of which I had only dreamed. More important, he was different from the type of person I usually met. When he asked me to go for a ride with him, it took all of about two seconds for me to accept. As we drove through town with the top down, I felt cool and deliciously carefree. I felt like a princess.

For the next couple of weeks, Joe and the rest of the crew hung out with my friends. Joe and I had really hit it off, and when he held my hand, I felt special. Here was a guy who probably met a lot of girls in his travels, yet he still wanted to be with me.

One night, after one of our drives in his convertible, I took Joe to a party given by some of the kids in my class. Joe looked especially handsome that night, and the opportunity to walk into the party on this hot guy's arm was too good to pass up. And indeed there were plenty of envious stares from the other girls; even the boys were staring at me, as if showing up with Joe had suddenly raised my attractiveness quotient.

For the next few hours, we had a great time, hanging out with my friends and listening to Joe's stories about the places he had worked. As I sat next to him on the couch, our hands intertwined, I felt like the queen of the world. I had even had a couple of beers, which is what kids do in small towns. But unlike many of my peers, alcohol had been introduced into my teenage rebellion later than others—I'd just had my first drink the summer before my senior year. But on that perfect warm spring night, I decided it wouldn't hurt to indulge a little. Sure enough, I started to feel a little tipsy, but I honestly didn't know if it was the drinks or the attentiveness of my date. Mostly I think I was intoxicated by the realization that it was possible to step out of my daily life and experience something else. This was a heady realization for someone who had grown up as I had.

The party was winding down when Joe leaned over and whispered that he wanted to be alone with me.

I nodded; then, still holding hands, we left the room in search of privacy. A few minutes later, we found ourselves in one of the bedrooms.

After shutting the door behind us, he wrapped his arms around me and placed a soft kiss on my lips. I kissed him back, giddily anticipating what I thought would be the best make-out session of my life.

Even as we made our way over to the bed, I couldn't believe that this guy was actually attracted to me, that he had chosen me over the other girls. I held that thought as we kissed, and even as he started fumbling with my clothes. When his hands started to roam, I just smiled and pulled them up, the universal hint for "that's off limits." He smiled too, and his hands stayed put for a while.

After a few minutes, though, the hands were traveling again, and his kisses were growing more insistent. He said to me, "I just want to see you. Take off your clothes." As a naïve girl, I obeyed. He stood up and pulled a silver package from his pocket. I quickly recognized it from health class, and it suddenly occurred to me that he thought we were there for more than just kissing. I panicked, as if awakening from a dream. I stood up quickly and said something about going back to the party, but he just smiled again and pulled me in close. I pulled back in earnest and said, "No, I can't"—and that was when everything changed.

In an instant my charming, friendly date was gone,

replaced by someone completely different. I tried to squirm away from him, but he just grabbed me tighter, pushed me back down on the bed, and stuck his tongue down my throat. I retreated to the floor, trying to crawl away and still trying to convince him that we needed to go back to the party. But my pleas fell on deaf ears. Feeling the first real bite of fear, I tried to push him off me again, but his body felt like a lead weight on mine.

"No!" I said again, pleading this time. "No, no, no, no, please no...."

Then I felt his steely grip around my throat. "Quit moving, or I'll hurt you." His voice was a snarl, nothing like the good-natured voice of Joe. The hand tightened just a bit, just enough to let me know he was serious. I could hear the others down the hall, talking and laughing, but I knew no one would be coming to save me. My body was frozen, my mind unable to comprehend what was happening to me, what he was doing. I was screaming in my head now, *No, no, no,* for fear that he would hurt me more if I made any noise. The little girl part of me was screaming, *Daddy, Daddy, help me!* while the grownup part was crying because I would no longer be a virgin on my wedding night. *I'm so sorry, Tim. I'm so, so sorry. Oh God, please make him stop. Please someone help me.*

After what seemed like an eternity, it was finally over. Still pinned beneath him, I lay there, shocked and terrified of what Joe might do next. My body was so drained of strength, I wasn't even sure I could move. My head felt all wet, and realized I had been crying so hard the tears had rolled down toward the floor, filling my ears like little pools.

The denial began the minute he rolled off me. *Nothing happened, nothing happened, nothing happened.* I thought it as he zipped up his pants; I thought it when he turned his face away as I got dressed, like a gentleman respecting my modesty. I thought it as he stood up and held out his hand to help me off the floor, and I thought it as he continued to hold it when we went out and sat down on the couch like any other couple. Something had snapped inside me, and I had flipped a switch, like a robot trying to convince myself this wasn't my reality. The crowd had thinned out, but there were still some kids talking and listening to music. If I ever had any doubt about my acting ability, they were squashed that night. Not one of these kids who had known me all my life had any idea that anything was wrong. And why would they? Nothing had happened, right?

Over the next couple weeks, *nothing happened* became my mantra. Joe's crew eventually finished up their work and left town, which only made my self-delusion easier to perpetuate. Shortly after that night, I reunited with Tim and resumed my role as a small-town high school student, obedient Christian, and virginal girlfriend. At the time I really believed I would be able to live out my life as if the rape hadn't happened; it never occurred to me to report it to the police or to anyone else for that matter. This was because underneath all the denial, I was already blaming myself for what had happened. But I couldn't face the look of disapproving repugnance I was convinced would be on people's faces when they found out. It was too much to bear when paired with my own guilt.

Unfortunately my secret was exposed much sooner and in a much more painful way than I could have imagined. The details are not important here, but suffice it to say that Tim learned the truth first. I realize now that although he was older than I was, he was still only twenty and had experienced the same sheltered upbringing. At the time, however, he had the worst possible reaction. Instead of comforting me for what I had been through, he was only able to focus on the fact that I had been to a party with another guy—an out-of-towner, no less—and had gone willingly with him to a bedroom.

In that instant I could no longer tell myself that nothing had happened. My façade crumbled, and all I could do was cry and beg for his forgiveness. What Tim did next was even worse—he insisted I tell my mother that very night. Too broken to argue, I agreed and waited for my mom to return from shopping. I guess he didn't trust me, because he followed me into the kitchen and made sure I confessed to Mom. Aside from the rape itself, this was probably the most humiliating experience of my life.

Mom's reaction was just as damaging, if not more so, than Tim's had been. I say this not as a condemnation; I know that as a mother she must have been in terrible pain when she heard what Joe had done to me. I also realize now that in many ways she was no more equipped to deal with a rape than Tim. Like me, she had grown up in a safe, little world where things like this didn't happen unless, of course, one went looking for them. Judging from her tone and the look on her face, she most certainly felt that I had gone looking for trouble when I had gone into that room with Joe. I wanted to explain how nice he had seemed and how he had made me feel when he took me driving or held my hand, but I knew how ridiculous it would sound. In truth I could barely remember those things myself. All I could remember was the snarl on his face and his fingers wrapped around my throat.

My mother's next words would change the course of my life.

"We will never tell your father about this."

For a moment I just looked at her, stunned. Not tell my father? My family had never kept secrets from each other before. Then it dawned on me: my mother thought this was all my fault, and she believed my father would feel the same. He would be disgusted with me. So I just nodded, completely devastated.

It wasn't that I *wanted* to tell Dad about the rape; the thought of it actually made me sick to my stomach. It was the nagging thought that if he knew, he wouldn't love me anymore. I knew what had happened, and if I couldn't love myself, how could I ever expect anyone else to do that? The term *damaged goods* was more real to me than anything I had ever known. Joe had stolen more than my virginity; he had stolen my very soul that night. I felt damaged in every aspect of my being. And I so longed for my dad to hug me and tell me everything was going to be all right. It was irrelevant, though, because I had promised my mother I would stay silent. It wasn't until my father died so suddenly that I realized I had been waiting for a perfect moment to tell him, to find out once and for all whether he could forgive me. When that chance was stolen from me, I bottled up my feelings until the fateful night in 2012.

As I walked in the door that night, pale and shaking from my botched suicide attempt, I knew it was time to tell my husband about my hell. He already knew about the rape, but he didn't know how much being damaged goods had eaten away at me for years. He sat there, quietly listening as I told him how I had been carrying the pain of the rape and feeling that I was unlovable not just by my father but by anyone. Jason was wonderful—

he could have yelled and screamed at me for nearly leaving him and the children, but he just listened without judgment as I unloaded decades of pain.

The next morning I awoke feeling like I had been run over by a train. Jason had graciously helped the kids off to school, and I ran a bath, thinking it would make me feel better. As I lay soaking in the warm, soapy water, I thought about all I had confessed to Jason—mainly that I had been blaming myself for the attack all those years ago. My mother and Tim had been right—it never would have happened if I hadn't been so naïve...so...

"*Stupid*," I muttered out loud, startling myself. "You were so stupid."

As I said the words over and over again, I felt this odd sense of relief washing over me, as if I were purging some unspoken thing that had been festering in my gut. "So stupid. You were an idiot last night."

That was when I realized that I didn't need forgiveness from my father or God. I had certainly asked his forgiveness plenty of times over the years, and as a Christian I believed he had granted it. Nonetheless when you don't feel deserving of the forgiveness, it doesn't seem to free you. The person I desperately needed to forgive me was *me*!

Feeling like a weight had been lifted from my heart, I said out loud, "I forgive you. I forgive you for being stupid. I forgive you for being naïve. I forgive you for being weak. I forgive you..." And on and on. I chanted it over and over, much like I had twenty years before, saying "Nothing happened." For every cruel thought I'd ever had about myself, I now offered my forgiveness.

An hour later, when I left that tub all wrinkled from the extended soak, I felt freer than I had since I was eighteen. I had found peace. The degrading thoughts and voices in my head had quieted. All I heard now was beautiful silence!

Questions to Ask Yourself

1. What do you do to avoid your negative emotions?
2. What is dragging your life down that you need to forgive yourself for?
3. Have you been avoiding taking responsibility for something?
4. From whom do you need to seek forgiveness?
5. What fears do you have that may be holding you back from forgiving?

CHAPTER 3

Foundation

A few months ago, I read a news story about Marine Sergeant John Peck, a young soldier who lost all four limbs while serving in Afghanistan in May 2010. He and another marine had just completed a routine knock-and-greet mission when Peck stepped on a bomb. As he lay on the ground, he felt the life draining out of him. He prayed he would live to make it back home.

When he woke up two months later, Peck found he had made it back to the United States. However "home" was now Bethesda Naval Hospital, where he would undergo twenty-eight agonizing surgeries. In one instant this strong, vibrant young man had gone from a warrior to someone who could not perform the simplest task for himself. As he faced the prospect of life without appendages, Peck understandably went through what he called "some very dark times." He pushed everyone away, including his wife, who eventually divorced him.

A few years later, however, he had pulled himself out of his depression and, quite simply, made a decision to live rather than just exist. He was eventually fitted with prosthetic legs and even went on Match.com, where he met a nurse who was moved by his courageous story. The two now have a son and are engaged to be married. Peck's next challenge? He is learning how to stand still (not an easy feat on prosthetic legs), to allow him to stand opposite his bride at the altar as they say their vows. After the wedding he will undergo a groundbreaking double arm transplant. From this point on, he must spend years learning to do everything from holding a cup to brushing his teeth.

I have had the privilege to know another such gentleman personally. We were kids together; we went to school together, played kickball together, and passed notes in the hall. Kevin Claussen was a great kid, well adored by our whole town. But one tragic hunting accident left the fourteen-year-old fighting for his life one crisp fall day in November 1988. He was rushed to the hospital with sheer minutes to spare. He immediately underwent one lifesaving surgery to repair his internal organs plus two reconstruction surgeries to rebuild his back and spent the next five months in the hospital.

My siblings and I were so excited for his release, we decorated his house and waited patiently to welcome our friend home. But Kevin's new reality was that he could no longer play kickball with us or run around the neighborhood playing tag. He would never be able to dunk a basketball the way his older brother could or dance with a girl at prom the same way everyone else did. You see, Kevin was now paralyzed from the waist down. However, even though this young man was wheelchair bound, he grew up determined to get the most out of life, never missing a beat when it came to school activities and community events. Kevin went off to college and landed a career with the Social Security Administration. He was married, and through the miracle of medicine they were able to have three beautiful children. This childhood friend just celebrated his fortieth birthday. Over the past twenty-six years, he has had six more surgeries for problems with pressure sores, each time leaving him hospital bound for up to five months. Needless to say he has overcome some extreme circumstances.

If you're like me, you're in awe of these men who overcame unspeakable pain and helplessness to become stronger than ever. As exceptional as they are, their stories are just two examples of millions of people who have risen above personal tragedy with seemingly inhuman physical, mental, and emotional strength. Even more incredible is that they don't just survive; they go after what they want in life with enviable passion, leaving the rest of us to wonder how in the world they did it. They seem to have an inner reserve of spirit, a flame that cannot be doused no matter what their circumstances. They have a *foundation*.

Foundations are important to everything in life, both tangible and intangible. When people go to buy a home, one of the first things they check is the foundation. And when a scientist comes up with a new hypothesis or a philosopher has a new theory, it must be based—founded—on something solid. The same is true of individuals—each of us needs a strong foundation on which to build our life. Without it we are like trees with weak roots: a storm will eventually come along and blow us over.

Most of us understand and grasp this fact, so then why do so many people feel like they are going through life without a rudder? The biggest reason is so many people build false foundations for themselves—usually around stuff. It is easy to get caught up in the desires to make more money and buy better things not just because we live in a materialistic society but investing in things feels safe. People can hurt you, people die, people leave—things never do. However, they cannot fill the void in your heart.

There is nothing wrong with chasing success as long as you put those aspirations in their proper place and refuse to let them define you. "Money is only money," my mom has always said. "It isn't the people in your life." Mom has given me a lot of great advice but none better than that. This brings me to my next point, which is the role of family in our life's foundation.

Family Is Our Original Foundation

Family is an essential part of our foundation. It is through our family that we first experience the world. The bonds we have with our parents and siblings will be instrumental in forming the basis for our relationships with friends, spouses, and children. Whether they are positive or negative, the memories we create with our family will stick with us for the rest of our lives. A strong family nurtures us, teaches us values, and offers us its support even when the rest of the world turns its back on us. A strong family makes us feel loved and secure—it gives us a foundation.

Most important, family shapes and molds us into who we are by giving us an example we want to emulate, one we want to reject, or a cross between the two. Whatever the case, family prepares us to strike out on our own. Good or bad, our family is our roots, and we need to make peace with and embrace them before we can become the best versions of ourselves.

As cultural norms have changed, so has the concept of family. Not too long ago, society's idea of family was a mother, a father, two and a half kids, and a dog; anything else was considered "less than." If someone's parents were divorced, they were said to come from a broken home. Being a single mother had all sorts of negative cultural and socioeconomic connotations. The woman was labeled irresponsible or worse, and the child spent his or her life overcoming the stigma. At one point the word *illegitimate* was even stamped on birth certificates!

These days the family unit is vastly different—it has changed along with the rest of our social norms. Some changes are considered progress while others seem to signify a breakdown in familial relationships. For example, roughly half of marriages end in divorce, which is certainly not ideal. The silver lining, however, is that children are no longer judged so harshly just because their parents split up. The relatively new *blended family* has replaced the more derogatory terms of the past. The same is true for single-parent homes— studies are divided on whether they impact children's educational and behavioral outcomes. However, many suggest children raised by one loving, well-adjusted parent are better off than those who grow up in a house with two dysfunctional parents.

The definition of extended family has also changed. In the past people did not move far from where they grew up. Sometimes they even remained in the same home with their parents and grandparents, where the multigenerational influence could be passed down and reinforce values. A slew of aunts, uncles, and cousins lived around the corner, creating a safe, secure world. Nowadays that lifestyle is the exception rather than the rule. Family members are spread out all over the country—even the world. They move away from home in search of better colleges, better jobs, and higher standards of living, keeping in touch largely through social media and text messages. However that does not diminish the fact that when the chips are down, your family will be there for you. They are still part of the foundation that supports you during life's struggles.

Family Is More Than Just Your Relatives

Right now you may be thinking, *That sounds all well and good, but you didn't grow up in a family like mine!* It's an unfortunate truth that many families fall far short of the ideal; in fact dysfunction, to varying degrees, has become the norm across all races, religions, and income levels. The important thing to remember is that even if you came from an unhappy home, you still have a foundation. If you think back, you'll recall someone from your childhood—a grandparent, family friend, or teacher—who cared for you, guided you, and tried to instill in you a sense of confidence. They may have done it overtly or by example; either way they provided a foundation you can continue to build upon throughout your life.

True family does not necessarily mean the family we were born into; they are the people we take into our inner circle. TV shows like *Friends* and *Sex and the City* are exaggerations of the urban family concept, but there is a seed of truth to them. We may have many acquaintances throughout our life; however certain friendships, when nurtured, can indeed become like the bonds of family. We share our pain and our joy with these people, tell them our most intimate secrets and hold their advice in high regard—just as we would with blood relatives. In return we encourage and expect them to honor us with the same degree of trust.

We need all the different people with all their different strengths in our life to have a strong foundation and really survive successfully. I have a supportive husband, family who love me, and twenty years' worth of friends in and out of my life. None of those people could give me the courage to face my deepest, scariest place in my life the way my friend Mark did. Without him I would still be running from my demons. Likewise, without Drew I would still be questioning my father's love.

Spiritual Foundation

A spiritual upbringing is another critical part of our foundation, one that ideally begins in childhood and is nurtured throughout our lives. Like family and school, spirituality provides children with structure; however it also teaches them the principles behind conducting themselves in a loving, honest manner. Through spirituality we learn that as children of God, all people deserve to be honored and respected, regardless of where they come from, how much money they've earned, or even when they've acted in a way of which we disapprove.

Like family, views on spirituality have shifted along with society. In fact these days, it is often dismissed as silly, unnecessary, even harmful in some cases, and so politically charged we are advised to avoid the topic at parties. Still, I believe our spiritual beliefs are vitally important to our sense of well-being and a critical part of our foundation. In difficult times, it can provide us with the kind of strength no one—not even family and friends—can provide. While spirituality is certainly not synonymous with faith, it does lay a foundation for faith and gives us a scriptural and historical context for it.

That being said, spirituality is not for everyone, and the freedom to worship or not worship as we wish is one of the founding principles of this country. But even if our parents chose to avoid raising us with spiritual issues present, that does not mean it cannot become part of our foundation. No matter how old we are or where we are on life's journey, we can choose to embrace a belief system that inspires us, enhances our faith, and reminds us there is a higher being watching out for us.

Building a Present Foundation

When I set out to write this book, one of the main points I wanted to express was that in order to move forward, we must learn to let go of our painful pasts. Part of doing this is realizing how the past has impacted our present and how we need to take responsibility for the decisions we make. In other words no matter what happened in the past or how shaky our foundation was while we were growing up, it is up to us to cultivate and nurture our present foundation with our spouses, friends, siblings and parents. It is a two-way street—if we want people to invest in us, we must invest in them.

We've all heard the expressions "talk is cheap" and "you can talk the talk, now walk the walk." However we don't really understand them until we are in the situation. How many times has someone promised you the world and then never acted on the promise? Or said they love you only to disappear when you needed them most? If you are being completely honest with yourself, you have probably done the same thing at one time or another. We all have—it's part of being human. The truth is words *are* important. They can wound or heal, and we must be careful how we use them. However there are many times when our actions mean so much more than what we say.

Ironically I learned this lesson after a fight with my husband. I believe that when you love someone, you should tell them all the time. Jason is not quite as vocal about his feelings. In my eyes it's just one of those things that makes a close relationship—particularly a marriage—an ongoing investment. It had always bothered me that Jason didn't say "I love you" as much as I did, and one night I let him know it. When I told him how hurtful it was, he was pretty confused. He didn't understand why I was getting so upset over words or lack thereof.

Finally, he said, "Shandy, I tell you I love you every night when I clean up after supper or give the kids their baths. If I didn't love you, do you think I would do that stuff?"

I didn't bother to tell him his response hurt my feelings even more than his silence had. Nonetheless I was thinking, *No, that's not love; that's just sharing life's responsibilities.* Then, a few weeks later, I saw him going into the boys' room. When I peeked in, I saw him battling the mountain of blankets and sheets I usually found on their beds. I realized Jason was getting everything in order so I wouldn't have to deal with it when I put them down to sleep. As I stood there watching him, I finally understood what he had said to me during the fight. True love is not in the words we say but in the unspoken—and often unappreciated—deeds we do without being asked. And yes, some of that stuff is shared responsibility, but that doesn't mean the actions are any less loving. I do those kinds of things for my family all the time; I just never noticed they were doing them for me as well. Seeing Jason act purely to help me was a wakeup call. We must pay attention to the actions of the people in our everyday lives. What loving deeds is someone doing for you? Better yet, what are you doing to acknowledge those deeds? You do need to acknowledge them if you want to maintain your foundation.

Some foundations are more difficult to maintain than others. For example, while the bond between parent and child is usually unbreakable, others, like marriages or friendships, are much more fragile. They must be continually nurtured and maintained if we want them to survive. Despite our efforts they can be shaky at times, especially during rough patches, like when someone has lost a job or is ill. That's why, just like faith and forgiveness, we must make the conscious decision to commit to the people in our lives. We might find ourselves having to renew our commitments on a daily or even hourly basis. What's more, we cannot just *say* we are committing; we must also act in a way that reinforces those commitments.

The above is easier said than done, especially when we feel burdened by life, and our foundation seems more like a prison than a haven. We've all heard those stories about the mother who cracks under pressure and drives off one day, never to be seen or heard from again. Like most people I've always been appalled by those stories—well, at least I am about ninety percent of the time. The other ten percent of the time, I can understand it. For example, after hearing my two-year-old son, Greyson, repeat a million times a day, "Mom, Mom, Mom…Mickey, Mickey, Mickey…Mom, Mom, Mom…Up, up, up." Hear that often enough and even the strongest soul can grow weary.

On one particular day, I had nearly reached my breaking point. I was the designated tax preparer, and with April 15 rapidly approaching, I knew I had to get started. I was dreading it; it was always a tedious affair. This year's return promised to be even more complicated than usual, largely due to our recent move to Omaha. Along with our usual business and living expenses, there was the sale of our old home and our moving costs. The night before, I had set my alarm earlier than usual, so I could get a jump on the paperwork before Greyson got up. Unfortunately that was also the morning my computer decided to go on the fritz. After ninety minutes of pressing keys and clicking the mouse and cursing technology altogether, I had printed exactly one page of the information I needed.

That was when Greyson woke up. My moments of solitude over, I decided to make the best of it by setting up a base of operations in the living room; that way I could work and keep an eye on my son. Needless to say, between coloring pages and resetting the DVR to Mickey, I didn't get much done, so I was grateful when my husband came home from work, a bag of take-out in hand. We would eat lunch, and he could watch Grey while I worked. Or so I hoped.

Sure enough, after we finished lunch, Jason snuggled up with Grey on the recliner, hoping to settle him down so he would take a nap. Determined to put my frustrating morning behind me, I turned back to the mountain of paperwork. To my dismay, a few minutes later, I heard that tiny voice again: "Mom, Mom, Mom….Mickey, Mickey, Mickey." When I looked over, I saw Jason was fast asleep; Greyson, however, was raring to go. He had crawled down and was heading my way, a determined look on his face. As tempting as it was to go over to the chair and shake my husband awake, I couldn't bring myself to do it. He had, after all, gotten up in the middle of the night for his grueling sales route. As if on cue, he began snoring—a sure sign he was exhausted. With a sigh I put down the form I was holding and snatched up my son. I held him until he drifted off to sleep and then once again returned to my work.

A glance at the clock told me I could still make some real headway on the taxes before the other kids got home from school. I shifted into high gear, spreading the piles of paper out on the floor and then organizing them into stacks of files and receipts. I was so absorbed in my task that I barely noticed the rhythmic cadence of Jason's snoring. A few minutes later, the snoring ended with two loud snorts; then came the sound of the television being turned on. Jason had awakened himself and was now looking around the room groggily, remote in hand.

I had my pencil poised over the form, trying to figure out where to put the personal property and state taxes. If you've ever done your own taxes, you know how hard it is to concentrate even in the best of conditions. I had been trying to do it while watching a toddler and dealing with a defunct computer. Jason's hunting show, blasting four feet away, was the final straw. Normally I would have just picked up and moved, but there was no way I was dealing with all those papers again now that I had finally gotten them organized.

I looked up at Jason and tried to keep the tension out of my voice. "Can you please go watch that downstairs? I can't concentrate on this stuff with the TV on."

If he had only said "sure" and gone downstairs, all

would have been fine. Instead he made a huffing noise, shot me an annoyed look, and stayed put. I just looked at him for a moment in disbelief; then I picked up the nearest form and began to read out loud: "All taxes charged under section 77-1317 shall be exempt from any back interest or penalty and shall be collected in the same manner as other taxes levied upon real estate..."

I paused when I heard Jason shifting in the chair, but when he didn't get up, I continued reading, a little louder this time, my finger keeping my place on the page. "Except for taxes charged on improvements to real property made after September 1, 1980. Interest at the rate provided..."

It worked! Visibly annoyed, Jason clicked off the TV...just as the three other kids walked through the front door. I decided to give up on taxes for the day since now it was time to help Logan with his homework. Sighing, I followed him to the kitchen table and tried to put a smile on my face. On a good day, helping with Logan's homework was about as much fun as getting wisdom teeth pulled. That day it was like the dentist had forgotten the Novocain, especially with the other kids running around, distracting Logan and causing a general ruckus. Jason heard me yelling and finally dragged himself from the PlayStation game he had been playing in the basement. To his credit he tried to help; he came upstairs to police the kids and then ran to the store to get supper groceries.

"Mom just needs a break for a bit before we eat," I announced as soon as he returned, then I went to draw a bath. The bathtub has always been a sanctuary for me—a place to decompress and wash off the stress of the day. Not this time! Greyson kept coming into the bathroom, repeating, "Mom, Mom, Mom... Up, up, up". I don't usually ignore my children, but in that exceptionally human moment, I really didn't care. I put my earbuds in to listen to symphony music and drown out the voice of my son—and the rest of my world. Finally he gave up and left the bathroom, and I sank deeper into the warm, soapy water.

A half hour later, I returned to the kitchen, hoping someone had started the spaghetti, but they were all way too busy bickering in the living room. Trying to salvage the calm from my bath, I kept my earbuds in. Still, as I dumped the pasta into the pot of boiling water and tied up the full trash bag, I felt that "had it up to here" feeling building behind my eyes. If you don't know what I'm talking about, ask any parent. He or she will tell you it is the sense of being completely trapped—a prisoner in your own life.

Suddenly it hit me: *I could just drive away!* Get into the car and stay in some quiet hotel room with zero responsibilities. In that moment I desperately wanted to do that with every fiber of my being. Instead I silently cried as I finished making dinner, set the table, and called everyone to eat. I did my best to act normal;

nonetheless I was still fighting back tears as I scooped some pasta onto everyone's plates. As I watched my family gobble down their food, I thought, *I don't want to be around* any *of you anymore! I can't stand any of you anymore!* I couldn't stop thinking of the car sitting in the garage and the keys in my purse.

The rest of the evening was no better. After several more mini dramas and tussles, I finally managed to get the kids to bed. It wasn't until later, when I was in my own bed at last, that the urge to flee passed. I realized why the mere thought of leaving had brought me some relief. It meant I had a choice. I could leave or I could stay. I chose to hold on to my family, my foundation. Sometimes it is easy to confuse nightmares with regular life. That day, as hellish as it seemed, was simply another day with kids. When we have families, our lives are no longer just about ourselves. The truth is that it's not even about our children. It is about "us" collectively making it through each day. It is an understanding that even when you are faced with the most infuriating, most overwhelming, most hated day, you must hang on to the "us" because the alternative is waking up alone.

Sure, the silence of that hotel room may seem glorious at first, but it would soon become deafening. You would experience an emptiness in your soul that all the freedom in the world would not fill. In that solitary moment, you would give anything just to have the family foundation, with all its chaos, back again. So while life can be very difficult in the moment, sometimes you must put aside your own wants and needs for the good of the "us." It is when you want most to cut these ties that you must work hardest to hang on to them.

As my dear friend Mark once said, "You are a strong person, Shandy, so fight! Fight for your marriage over everything else in life, and you will never regret it." Marriage is part of the foundation that sustains you during the hard times and shares your joy when things are going well. It will help you beat back your nightmares and hold you accountable for your life. The benefits of a fully invested marriage are immeasurable.

Building Foundations for the Future

Even as we work to maintain our past and present foundations, we must also be looking ahead to the foundations we'll build in the future. This comes into play when we are thinking about having children. As a mother of four (and someone who grew up with a very strong family foundation), I can tell you nothing you will do in your life will be as important as building a foundation for your kids. As they grow, they will rely on this foundation to guide them in their decision making and enable them to reach their full potential.

Again, I am not saying this flippantly. It is not easy

to build a strong foundation for your children. To do so you have to be willing to put aside your own desires and do what's best for them not just in the moment but in the long term. Parenthood, even for the strongest among us, is the hardest job in the world. It is also the longest. Your kids never stop being your kids. It doesn't matter if they are age six, sixteen, or sixty—you still worry about them and want to protect them from the dangers of the world. The best thing we can do as parents is become very clear as to who we are and, whenever possible, behave in alignment with the lessons we are trying to teach.

To many new parents, the weight of this responsibility comes as a shock. When we're young we often feel powerless over our lives. Every decision—what we eat, what time we go to sleep, where we go and with whom—is made by someone else. Our mothers and fathers are omniscient and always in control, and we can't wait to grow up so we too can do whatever we want. It is not until we reach adulthood, with all its burdens and responsibilities, that we see the error in our thinking; and it is not until we have our own children that we realize parents are just people dealing with their own baggage, hurts, and unmet needs. We are not suddenly infused with some greater awareness the minute our children enter the world. We don't always know what we are doing; in fact we often feel as lost as our kids.

"All you can do is try your best," my mother always

says. "Go with your instincts, and turn them over to God, so he can do the rest."

We won't always know how to deal with a bad situation in the best way. My mother didn't handle the news of my rape the best way; however I know without a doubt that she did the best she could at that moment. She was completely blindsided by the news. She had no training on how to deal with victims of sexual assault. She had lived her entire life in a safe community where things like rape didn't happen (or if they did, they weren't talked about). Her gut reaction was to do what was necessary to protect the family unit.

Parents might also have a hard time expressing their emotions. This goes back to their foundations growing up. For example, if a young boy grows up with an aggressive, domineering father, there is a good chance he will be the same kind of parent—unless he learns to channel anger in a more productive way. By the same token, people who grow up in homes with little affection may have difficulty expressing love and affection to their own spouses and/or children.

When I was growing up, my father didn't always do the best job at making me feel he loved me (although to be fair, he did tell me he did all the time). Like my mother he was doing the best he knew how given his own upbringing and experiences. He had no idea that the way he interacted with me would later influence not only my relationship with my husband but also my children. There was no Internet back then, no easily accessible parenting articles. Yet the truth of it is that my relationship with my father shaped every aspect of my life; it even impacted my ability to deal with the rape and find peace after he died.

After years of struggling with these feelings, two well-timed conversations with Drew helped me put everything into perspective. Drew was on a mission to convince me that my father would have loved me no matter what I had done or what had happened to me.

"But how can you possibly know that?" I asked him during one of our marathon conversations after my suicide attempt.

"I know this because my old man tells me this all the time. No matter what I do, he still loves me and is proud of me, and if *my* old man can say this, then I know without a doubt that your dad would have felt the exact same way about you."

Drew had some credibility in this department, as he had known my father quite well. Still, I didn't really believe him at the time. All I kept thinking was that no one would ever know what Dad would say until we got to ask him in heaven. Two years later Drew was going through a really rough period. There was even one particularly crazy weekend when he had messed up in front of one of his church's leaders and his parents, who were justifiably mortified. The next weekend was Memorial Day; he picked up his dad to take his usual stroll through the cemetery. For the first time ever, Drew lit up a cigarette in front of his father, which in his church was a big no-no. Thinking his father would be angry for his recent behavior, Drew was shocked when instead his dad grabbed his hand and said, "You may not be perfect, but you're perfect to me!" When Drew told me the story, I realized what he had said about my father had to be true as well. My dad would have said the same thing!

A girl's relationship with her father is unequivocally the most important relationship in her life; it is a blueprint for her subsequent relationships with men and therefore a critical part of her foundation. Whether she is conscious of it or not, there is nothing more important to a girl than the love and approval of her father. If she gets it, she will grow up with a strong sense of self-worth and will seek out relationships that reflect this back to her. If she fails to receive that emotional connection with her father, she may spend years searching for love, acceptance, and validation from other men. Unfortunately there are millions of men out there who will gladly take advantage of that weakness. So to all the men who are reading this book, be strong for your daughters. No matter how uncomfortable you may feel about expressing your feelings, you must find a way to overcome the discomfort. Tell her she's smart, beautiful, and deserving of respect. Most important, hug her and tell her you love her no matter what she could ever do. You will never be sorry you did. She, on the other hand, will be very sorry and sad if you don't.

I've gotten a lot of great advice on parenting over the years. Most of it has come from my mother, but one of my aha moments came from an old high school classmate, Daphne, who said:

"It is hard watching our babies grow up. We remember holding them right after they were born, and while they don't have that memory, that image will stick with us forever. I'm convinced that is one reason it's hard to let go. We also know of the hurts and dangers that lurk around the corner. If we look at it from a child's point of view…they don't have all of these fears because they don't have our knowledge. You know that saying 'ignorance is bliss'? Well, it's true. Remember how you are raising your children and what kind of role models you are for them. They are drinking in all you are offering even if you don't see them at the cup."

I have never forgotten those words, even after we moved to Omaha and my fears about the dangers "lurking around the corner" multiplied. When you're a parent, the need to protect your babies sometimes takes over and casts a shadow on everything else. Part of your job is making sure your kids are safe; however in each situation you must be able to take a step back and assess whether you are protecting them or indulging your own hang-ups. For example, each time I saw another crime story on the news, I desperately wanted to pack my children up and move them as far from the city as possible. Had I done that, however, not only would I have protected them from potential harm; I also would have taken away valuable opportunities.

Parents also want to protect their children from emotional wounds. Again, it is important to be discerning here. Children learn through experience, and if we step in to protect them from pain, they will never learn to process their emotions or make healthy choices moving forward. When I was raped, my mother tried to protect my father and me by keeping it a secret from him. In doing so, she figured, she was sparing my feelings in the event that he judged me for what had happened. She was trying to help, but in the end the secrecy was more harmful to me than the rape itself. It bred shame and fear that my father couldn't love me anymore.

Sometimes it is better to make choices that are uncomfortable in the moment but will be healthier in the days to come. When hurtful things are processed in an honest and productive way, children learn to handle future challenges in the same manner. It is helping them build a strong foundation.

What Can You Do to Strengthen Your Foundation?

Whether we realize it or not, each of us has the strength to deal with the worst life can throw at us; however we cannot do it alone. Some of us inherit our strength from the family into which we are born. Others find it in our friends or in God. Some of us are lucky to have gained it from all of these things! Whatever the case everyone can do something to strengthen their foundation. Take a moment to recognize the people who have your back, and consider what you can do today to show your appreciation for them. Also make an effort to give back and show support for someone else.

We can also strengthen our foundation by investing time in people outside our inner circle. These are the folks we interact with during the course of our day, and while we may not confide in them or even know their names, they can bring gifts to our lives if we pay attention. As someone who has worked with the elderly, I can attest to the fact they are a great, untapped source of wisdom. Our senior citizens are the foundations not only of our families but of our society as a whole. They are links to another time, and they have lifetimes of experience and wisdom to share with us if we would only take the time to talk to them. Yet all too often I see people dismissing the elderly as burdensome or irrelevant. Think of the perspective an eighty-year-old has on life—both its struggles and its blessings. The elderly have the power to help us refocus our energies on what's truly important. In return we can give them an invaluable gift: our time. When we interact with elderly people, whether they are related to us or not, we reconnect with all that's good about past generations. It is a win-win.

I have been reminded of this valuable lesson many times. One specific time was when I went to a nursing home to give an eight-hour training on dementia. It was an enjoyable day but a long one, and I still had to attend my daughter's fifth-grade concert that night. It was the last one of the school year, and, not wanting to be late, I'd planned on rushing away as soon as my presentation was over.

One of the nursing home's residents, however, had other ideas. I was hurrying down the hall with my arms full with all my necessary props when a man came out of his room and asked me for a piece of paper. Inwardly groaning, I put everything down and handed one to him. He smiled and then stood there watching as I packed all my stuff back up. I was just about to leave when he said, "Can I have two?"

At that point I really wanted to mumble an excuse and continue on my way, but I couldn't bring myself to do it. Instead I put everything back down again, dug into my tote, and got out another piece paper. He waited for me to pick up my stuff again before asking, "Do you have a pen?"

Oh what the heck, I thought as I dug into my purse. *I'm late anyway, right?* I handed him the pen and then stood there for a moment, convinced the minute I packed everything up he would ask for something else.

But he didn't. Instead he smiled and said, "Thank you. I want to write a story about you. You're a great person."

As he said that, I felt a rush of emotions that included a twinge of guilt that I had wanted to get away from him earlier. Mostly I felt like I had been given two gifts. The first was his kind words, and the second was the realization that I had almost missed them because I was in a hurry. Sometimes we avoid people we think are not worth our time, but this is a mistake. More often than not, when we invest our time and attention in someone, they reciprocate tenfold in one way or another.

In another instance a woman from my church asked if I would sing at a nursing home. It would be for only fifteen minutes, but fifteen minutes is a lot of time when you're a working mother of four. I wanted to say no, but when I checked my schedule and realized I did not have a reasonable excuse, I shrugged and gave her a half-hearted "OK, sure." I must admit other than marking the date and time on my calendar, I didn't give my upcoming performance much thought. I barely practiced, thinking it wouldn't matter anyway. I figured old people were safe—they wouldn't judge me. Heck, some of them wouldn't even hear me! I didn't even arrange for childcare for my son, Greyson, who was nearly two at the time. When the day arrived, I just packed the diaper bag and headed over to the nursing home.

When I got there, a staff member directed me to the lunchroom, where some of the residents had gathered to hear me sing. Balancing my son on my hip, I stood at the front of the room and looked out at my audience— elderly men and woman at various stages of mental and physical health. Each of them was someone's mother, father, grandparent, or spouse, yet they were all there, living out their final years in that place. And they were staring at me, waiting to be entertained.

So for a quarter of an hour, I sang my songs, adding some inspirational words to each one. Well, my performance must have been acceptable because as I was preparing to leave, the residents started cheering. One man who could barely speak yelled out, "God bless you, angel!" To this day I am not sure who got more out of those fifteen minutes—them or me. The experience left me feeling inspired, appreciated, and most of all truly blessed.

So whether it is your spiritual foundation, your family foundation, or your past, present, or future foundation that is your strongest, all of our foundations are important and necessary to us in surviving nightmares. Just like the foundation of a house is very important and necessary to the building, they give us our strong footing upon which to build our home. Storms may come along and wipe out our house, but we will always have that strong foundation left on which to rebuild.

The same concept is repeated in our lives. Sometimes the nightmares seem to wipe out everything we have clung to or held as important, but if our foundation is strong, we will be able to rebuild our life. Hopefully we can build a bigger and better life than before because we learned from the storm how to live life better.

Questions to Ask Yourself

1. Who is in your family foundation?
2. What loving deeds is someone doing for you? What are you doing to acknowledge those deeds?
3. What specifically can you do to strengthen your foundation?
4. What fears do you have that you do not want to pass down to your children?
5. Can you think of a time when a stranger blessed your life in a memorable way?

CHAPTER 4

Fun

A recent poll by Gallup and Global Healthways named Panama as the happiest country in the world. The poll encompassed 135 countries and surveyed 133,000 people based on five factors: community, physical environment, financial, purpose in life, and social contentment. The Panamanians were thriving in four of the five categories. The numbers indicated strong family values, and spending time with family regularly, rather than sending texts and Facebook messages, was a primary source of happiness and contentment.

As members of a very different, much more type-A society, we might wonder why Panama was rated so high on the happiness scale. Panama was easily surpassed by other countries when it came to finances; in fact money was the one factor in which the small South American country received a low score. This thought process may be difficult to reconcile with our way of thinking, when our lives are often filled with paying bills and making sure our kids have the latest iPad or whatever brand of sneaker is in that year. Essentially Panamanians possess a lot less than the average American, so where does the happiness come from?

When the statistics were compiled, one conclusion stood out: they had more fun than we did. Their fun was not based on possessions; it was based on the simple enjoyment of life shared with each other. When you look at your life with this perspective in mind, are you having fun?

Remember when you were a kid, and having fun was as natural as breathing? Have you ever wondered what happened to that kid or when the last time was you truly enjoyed yourself? If so you are not alone. During childhood our essential needs were probably taken care of by the adults in our lives, leaving us unfettered and full of creative energy. We had endless curiosity about the world. There were opportunities for fun everywhere we looked. In fact much of our growing-up years were spent in a tug-of-war with our parents and teachers, with us trying to soak up more fun and with them trying to curtail our fun so we could do our homework, clean our rooms, and get enough rest.

Somewhere along the line, we became less concerned with having fun and more concerned with the business of adulthood—getting a degree, landing that big job, and putting money in our 401(k). In our minds fun was replaced with more responsibilities and acquisitions, such as cars, homes, clothes, and the latest electronic gadgets. Our lives became all about hitting certain benchmarks—marriage, kids, career—rather than savoring our present reality of incorporating fun into our everyday lives. We began to gauge our happiness by how much we'd accumulated or how successful we were rather than by how much enjoyment we took in simple pleasures—and in each other. Fun was delegated to the weekends, when we could sleep in and have a few drinks with our friends. We started to shift our identity and fun experiences to coincide with our kids' experiences. We relished and relived our childhoods through their accomplishments and triumphs. Before we knew it, they were grown and we didn't know how we lost the fun in our lives. People start looking forward to retirement or grandkids, where they hope to find that fun again.

And we wonder why we often feel so unfulfilled! It sounds to me like we could all take a cue from the Panamanians. Whether we are trying to heal ourselves or just trying to enjoy life more, we could all use more fun in our lives.

Fun Can be Work, and Work Can Be Fun

Like all the other lessons in this book, I learned (sometimes the hard way) that fun is something to which we must commit. It is easy to get swept up in the whirlwind of everyday life—waking early, getting the kids off to school, and racing off to work while our mind is teeming with a never-ending to-do list. I am not suggesting we shirk our responsibilities, just that we acknowledge the need to incorporate fun into each day—even if only for a few minutes. Think of it as a conscious decision to nurture your spirit, just as you nurture your body with food.

How do you do this? Well, for starters, don't stress yourself out trying to find something fun to do. Chances are it is probably right under your nose, so don't make judgments about what you enjoy—just get out there and do it. There are as many ideas about fun as there are people on this planet. For some it is traveling to exotic locales, with white, sandy beaches; sparkling, blue water; tradewinds rustling through the thick, lush palm trees; and all the cares and stresses of life carried effortlessly away on the ocean's tropical breeze. Piña colada in hand equals paradise.

For others it might be simply a week's worth of splashing and laughing with the kids in the backyard pool. Everyone happy and healthy and just chillin'. Snapple with lemon equals bliss.

For some others fun might be having coffee with a friend, walking on the beach, or reading a book. Believe it or not, many people take pleasure in their work. We've all heard the saying "find something you love to do, and you'll never work a day in your life." This seems to be supported by the happiness poll, which found wealthier countries ranked lower due to their people's dissatisfaction with their work.

Now, I know everyone can't leave a job they hate and switch to one they consider fun; nevertheless everyone can find something in life that excites their soul and sparks life into their heart. This can be something creative, like artwork or woodworking, or it can be doing something that gives back to others, like my work in the nursing homes.

The most important job you will ever have is making memories with your family, whether that means your spouse and children or a bunch of friends. Pull out that smartphone and take photos as often as you can, not just on holidays. Those pictures are what will cement those events into your memory forever.

Seek Out Healthy Fun

It can be easy, especially for young people, to confuse fun with a need to fit in. In their desperation to connect with others and make friends, they may engage in behaviors that are not only unhealthy but can connect them with toxic people and lead them down the wrong path. They might drink, use drugs, or have sex before they are ready or with people who don't care about them. They may even join other kids in cruel activities such as bullying. They'll tell people they are having fun; nonetheless what they're really doing is going along with the crowd—anything not to be alone. When this happens the fun is not healing but something from which you need healing.

Most kids use fun as a way to rebel against the authority figures—parents, teachers, churches, and anyone else that exerts control over their lives. To some extent pushing back against these authority figures is a normal part of growing up. That being said, it is important to know the difference between fun that pushes the envelope and fun that endangers our physical, mental, and spiritual well-being.

Others use fun as an escape from pain. It often begins harmlessly enough, drinking in high school, indulging in the occasional joint in college, perhaps hanging out with some unsavory folks because they throw the best parties on campus. Then we figure out that these things make us numb to the things bothering us, whether they are on the forefront of our mind or are demons lurking below the surface. That's when having fun becomes an excuse for self-medicating away our pain. Once again I am speaking from personal experience. In college I used partying as a coping mechanism, not only so I could forget about the rape, but so I could feel normal again. When I was hanging out with the kids in my dorm, drinking and laughing, I could pretend I was like any other coed rather than the damaged, broken person I was hiding. When I looked in the mirror, I did not like what I saw, and drinking blurred that reflection. Like all victims I needed something to make me feel good again—something I could not find inside myself.

As I mentioned earlier, I also spent many years drinking myself through the pain of my father's death. While I told myself I was having fun drinking those beers, I was really trying to drown the pain of losing him. It was when I made the conscious decision to rebuild my life into something I wanted and deserved that the *real* fun began—the fun of healing.

You might be thinking, *Well, that doesn't sound like much fun—I'll stick with the beer!* To be truthful the healing process itself is *not* fun, not at all! But just like a long, frustrating line at the airport, it was the necessary first step. Before I could get on the proverbial plane, I had to go through all the appropriate checkpoints to arrive at my future.

I see that future every night in the faces of my four beautiful children as I tuck them into their beds and softly kiss them good night. I feel it every day in the loving touch of my husband. No exotic island, not even a backyard pool needed. The fun comes when you feel whole again and are able to appreciate the wonders you have every day in your life.

Fun—A Daily Dose

Fun is like the battery charger of life—it is necessary to motivate us and keep us moving forward. When we dismiss the fun stuff as frivolous or skip it because we are too busy or too tired, that's when we start to get burned out on life. You start feeling down again, like you're stuck in quicksand. That's the result of eliminating or ignoring the things that make you feel alive inside.

Incorporating fun into my everyday life has made an immeasurable difference in my spiritual, emotional, and physical well-being. I have also been committed to teaching my kids to place a high value on fun and to distinguish healthy fun from risky behaviors. I try to schedule at least one fun thing to look forward to each week. They are not usually large or expensive things—in fact I make an effort to find fun and excitement in the little moments. For example, my kids love to eat by candlelight, so I'll turn a simple supper into a fancy event with a few well-placed votives. Another thing I've done is serve a meal with toothpicks instead of silverware. It may sound silly, but watching my kids' faces as they do something new and different, maybe even a bit silly, is precious.

And make sure as a married couple you remember to have fun together as well as having fun with your kids. Having fun with the one you love keeps the spark alive not only in your soul but in your commitment to each other.

Create Fun in the Midst of Chaos

Remember even when life seems like a mess, and we can't find any real reason to have fun, we need to seek fun. Those are the times when we need fun the most. Children can help us do this. Making kids smile or creating exciting, fun things for little ones to do is something that brings me so much happiness. When life feels overwhelming, that's the exact time we need to go out of our way to seek out fun and attempt to smile.

In the midst of our move last summer, our living room was empty, as all of our furniture was packed in the moving van. Our bedrooms were cold and empty; just the beds were left. Our once loving home felt so hollow and vacant. Sadness was all around us, and I was really struggling to keep the tears from flowing.

I knew I had to turn the sadness around and decided to make something fun to brighten our morale. We set up our big, two-room tent in the living room and had a campout that night. We let our kids have the neighbors over, and there was happiness and laughter in the house once again. This in turn made my soul happy and brought a smile to my face again.

Laughter Can Truly Be Life's Best Medicine

It is important to be able to laugh and be silly some-times. It helps us look at life's problems in a little bit different light. Laughter is a release of emotions in the same fashion as crying is—we need both to be happy, healthy, successful people. Two of the things that attracted me to my husband were his wonderful sense of humor and his ability always to stay youthful. He had the ability to lighten my mood and teach me to view life less seriously.

I also turn to Drew when I start seeing too much darkness creep into my life. When things look bleak, I schedule some time to give Drew a call. He can always make me laugh. After a good phone conversation and a side-splitting laugh, I always feel as if my dark clouds have parted, and I am able to feel the sun shine down again.

The lesson here is: don't let your life get dull or gloomy. When it does, people have a tendency to start thinking, *Is this all there is?* Many people hit midlife and get wrapped up in parenting and careers, homework and budgets, school sports and overtime. We look in the mirror one day and say, "Is this it?" If and when we ask that question, we look outside our world to ignite our life again. Sometimes we look at things to cure our negative thoughts or to other people to fix our restless life. Those fixes are short term and in some cases even devastating to a marriage.

When we take all of this into account, the Panamanians have the right idea—sometimes making the most out of life and having fun is as simple as finding contentment in what we already have. Learn to celebrate life and find the joy of having fun every day— one day at a time, one fun time after another. Only then is there a chance for joy and excitement to return to our life.

Questions to Ask Yourself

1. How do you incorporate fun into your life?
2. Identify some unhealthy fun that has been part of your life.
3. What are three things you think are fun? When was the last time you did one of them?
4. Can you think of a time in your life when things seemed so overwhelming, you just busted out laughing? How did it feel?
5. What was the last thing you did that was fun with your spouse or loved one? How long ago was it?

CHAPTER 5

Forever

Webster's definition of forever is "without ending" or "for everlasting time." For humans this concept can be a bit paradoxical when we look at life. The fact that human beings have a beginning and an end on this Earth lends to this confusion. Life as we know it and everything we do while we are here has a beginning and an end. We want that same result when we are dealing with our nightmares in life. We are well aware they had a beginning, and we would like them to have an end. We want to be able to close that chapter in our life and put it away on a shelf where it will stay forever. Unfortunately this is not the way most nightmares work.

True Healing Is a Forever Process

Most of us are under the impression healing happens all at once and lasts forever. We have our demons, we exorcise them, and we are magically healed. The truth is healing is a process and, as the saying goes, a journey rather than a destination. It begins with one foot in front of the other and continues until the day we die. The good news is the journey gets easier the longer we are on the path of healing. Eventually the path even leads the way to a happy, healthy, successful life.

When I was four, while at my grandmother's house, I took one of my grandpa's toothpicks, stuck it in my mouth (as I had seen him do), and began running around the house with it. At some point, it fell out of my mouth and got caught in the blue shag carpet. However, being a four year old, I was on to something else and didn't bother to pick it up. Consequently, on my next pass through the room, my bare foot came squarely down on the strong, sharp wooden object. When Mom and Grandma heard me crying, they came in and found me clutching my foot. Promptly they got a tweezers and pulled the toothpick out. Lovingly they wiped away my tears and gave me one of Grandma's famous cookies, and all was good again.

At least so we thought. What they didn't know was at least an inch of it was still in my foot. It wasn't bothering me anymore, and with a child's buoyancy I was soon running all over the place again. We all were completely oblivious to the fact there was a sliver of wood still in my foot that would eventually park itself against my heel bone. It remained there for almost six months.

My body dealt with this foreign object by attempting to cover it with a calcium deposit. This only made the problem worse. After about five months of playing, running, and putting weight on it, my foot became so tender I could no longer walk normally. Most kids would have complained to their mother by that time, but not me! I was petrified of doctors (probably some repressed memory of the near-death experience I'd had when I was still an infant). I just turned my ankle and learned to walk on the side of my foot. I managed to fool my mother for about another month (no easy feat). Finally one day she noticed my strange gait and took me to the doctor. Sure enough, an X-ray revealed the rest of the toothpick.

Obviously, my mother was shocked when she found out what was causing my discomfort. She was even more shocked when the doctor announced it would require surgery to remove the toothpick. That tiny piece of wood had, over time, become dangerous to my well-being.

The point of this story? The longer we wait to deal with our problems, the more likely they are to fester and cause us a world of hurt later. Unfortunately we cannot always have our emotional toothpicks surgically removed. However if we are brave, we can steadily dig them out bit by bit. This excavation can be an extremely long and painful process. Nonetheless it is much less painful than waking up one day at the end of life's journey and dealing with regret, realizing all the years you wasted on repression and living a false life when you should have been enjoying life.

Scars Come from Nightmares

I have a three-inch scar on the side of my right foot to this day, reminding me of that toothpick. Scars happen when we endure something traumatic as well. Even when you have faced your demons and believe yourself to be rid of them, you will carry the scars of your battles.

Very few of us get through this life unscathed. Once our demons lose their ability to control our lives, we start to see those battle scars. We can then see them as signs of our strength and survival rather than signs of our weakness. You will still have bad days and trigger points. After all, you are a human being, not a robot. It does not mean you are failing; it just means there are more feelings for you to work through. The worst thing you can do when an event or person triggers a painful memory is shut down. Remember, keeping your emotions under wraps is what allowed your demons to flourish in the first place.

As I said earlier, writing this book was part of my healing process. It stands to reason it triggered a few setbacks along the way. For example, one day my husband and I were discussing the book as we pushed our cart around Walmart. He was asking me questions about some of the life events I was describing in the pages. With the progression of the conversation, the subject turned to the rape. As it turned out, something I had always considered a small detail not worth mentioning turned out to be a rather big deal to him. In the middle of the frozen food aisle, he gave me the most hurtful look. I had seen that look before, twenty-two years ago, the night Tim found out—the look of disapproving repugnance. It was a look that said, "Well, maybe you deserved it," or at least that was how I interpreted it in my head.

In truth the look probably didn't mean I deserved it per se; it was more a look of surprise that at eighteen years old I was naïve or stupid enough to put myself in a position to "let" something like that happen. It was undoubtedly the same look countless rape victims have gotten when people hear they wore skirts that were "too short" or that they danced provocatively or flirted in such a way.

Whatever Jason meant by the look, it took me right back to the night the rape happened. All those years of hard-won healing fell away once again to reveal brokenness and shame underneath. Without a word I stalked out of the store. Jason left the cart and ran after me, calling my name in the Walmart parking lot. I really couldn't hear him over the voice screaming in my head.

"See?" it said. "See? You *are* worthless! You asked for all of this, and you deserved it!"

I felt raw and exposed, and as angry as I was at Jason I was angrier at myself. After all that time, one look could take me right back to this dungeon. However, by the time I walked home something incredible had happened. My old defense mechanism had kicked in. I had completely shut down. I felt absolutely nothing! It was such a relief to have that pain gone. Actually I had no thoughts in my head whatsoever. All I could do was sit in a chair and blankly stare out the window.

When Jason got home and saw me sitting there, he asked if he should leave.

"Why?" I replied. "I feel nothing, and besides, why should you get a reward by leaving all the responsibilities of four kids behind you? I'm *fine!*" That was a phrase I had come to know so well over the years.

He didn't say anything, but I know he must have felt terrible about the look he had given me and disturbed by my reaction to it. We muddled through the night, managing to fake it through supper to avoid the kids' knowing something was wrong. Shortly thereafter, everyone went to bed—everyone except for me. That's when the demons come to call: at night, when you're alone in the dark, and your numb heart struggles to keep beating against the heaviness of your chest.

Suddenly it hit me! If I let the demons back in, I would be no more. I would never again get the upper hand—they would control me forever. The only way to keep the demons away was to feel the pain. In that moment I knew I couldn't run, I couldn't drink it away, I couldn't do anything except make myself feel whatever was coming to the surface. So I stopped fighting, I put on a song that spoke to my soul, and I *cried*.

Now, for some people crying is no big deal; some people even enjoy the release of a good cry. Not me. So imagine how shocking it was to my brain that I was actually allowing, even making myself cry. It felt incredibly strange at first, like the ultimate loss of control. I played tug-of-war with my thoughts on this strange, newfound way to cope. Nonetheless I refused to block it. As I cried, I realized that as upset as I was by the thought Jason was judging me, I was more upset that after so many years, I was still judging myself.

I cried until I was completely drained of energy. Then I crawled into bed, closed my eyes, and slept like a baby. The next morning I woke up feeling better—lighter—than I had in a long while. The trigger had resulted in an agonizing night, but it had also led me to another breakthrough. Life isn't about distracting ourselves from the painful things that have happened. It is about absorbing each and every moment and understanding the gifts these breakthroughs bring. As I like to say, great obstacles bring great fear and require great determination but ultimately bring greatness! Overcoming obstacles is the only way to turn life's nightmares into life's dreams.

Some people, when going through tough times, tend to make a show of strength when they feel anything but strong. For people like me, the weaker we feel, the greater the front we present to the world. This may be an excellent strategy in wartime, when a floundering army is using bravado to trick the enemy, but in everyday life nothing good comes from pretending we are invincible when we are falling apart inside. This sort of martyrdom ruins marriages and leads to addictions and, in my case, an attempted suicide on a dark, lonely road. Sometimes it is in showing our vulnerability to those around us that we truly display strength of character. There is nothing scarier than allowing others to see our demons and facing the conundrum of whether they will love us anyway.

The same concept applies if you are helping someone else deal with a crisis. When you hear about someone's experiences, and you don't know how to deal with them, or they make you uncomfortable, do not ignore them or sweep them under the rug. If you do, you may actually be doing more damage to the person. If you do not know what to say, be honest about it. Just be sure to acknowledge their pain and help them understand you will be there for them in any way you can.

Don't Hold Back

Part of "forever" is letting your loved ones see the real you, even those less-than-flattering sides. This can be scary, especially for people carrying a lot of shame and those feeling unlovable. They are always on guard to prevent saying something that sends the other person running for the hills.

We've all heard people say, "I wish I could have told so and so how much he or she meant to me" or, "I never got a chance to say..." This is exactly the place in which I found myself after my father died and where I would remain for a decade, haunted by all the things I had never expressed to him. I can personally attest to the fact that *nothing* is as painful as the words we've left unsaid.

I spent most of that decade blaming myself for not telling him about the rape; fortunately I have since forgiven myself for this. Young, terrified, and ashamed, I was not in an emotional place back then to make a different choice, especially since I thought it might cause him to see me differently. If I am being honest, my father's ignorance made it easier for me to forget the incident. In the back of my mind, I believed I would tell him when the time was right; it never occurred to me I could lose him so suddenly and never get to that perfect time.

His tragic death taught me a very valuable lesson: let your family and friends know you love them, and, even more important, let them know *you* now. Don't wait for when the time is right. The next time you are holding something back, ask yourself, "If this person were gone tomorrow, what unspoken words would I regret not saying?" Then take a few deep breaths, summon the courage to say whatever it is you need to say, and say it. Trust me, the fear of their reaction is nothing compared to the lifetime of regret if you don't say it.

This does not mean everyone is always going to agree with or even understand what we say, but this is not the goal. It is about sharing ourselves with the people we love and knowing they will support us no matter what. During one particularly frank conversation with Mark, I tried to explain to him my feelings of brokenness and why they often led me to do things that were, let's say, less than positive. He listened without interrupting me.

"Do you understand?" I asked finally.

"No," he replied, "but I love you enough not to have to understand."

This was one of those breakthrough moments I'll

never forget. I had expended so much energy trying to appear as though I had it all together, even to my friends and family. I had always been afraid they could never understand how I felt. It never occurred to me it didn't matter whether they understood or not—they would stand by my side regardless. The point is I never would have received this precious gift if I hadn't had the courage to confide in my friend.

It has taken me many years of self-destructive behavior to realize one simple truth: it is normal and natural to have emotions that are negative, positive, and everything in between. When we squash or bury or distract ourselves from our emotions, they become like that toothpick—a festering wound that will require more invasive treatment in the end. We all hurt, and that's okay. It's better than okay, in fact. If we allow ourselves to feel the hurt, then we can also allow ourselves to feel the love. To feel *anything* means we are alive and well.

Well now, what does *forever* mean? To me it means that recovering from trauma is an ongoing journey, with many twists, turns, and setbacks. It is often a "two steps forward, one step back" process, one you can evaluate only by gauging the overall trends of your moods and relationships. Telling my story has been a critical part of my healing process, for it has helped me drag those demons out of the darkness of my mind and into the light, where I could confront them head-on. This includes all the things society insists we keep hush-hush. These are things like rape or depression, which even to this day carry such a bad stigma people would rather suffer in silence than let people see inside their hell. We refer to these things as the skeletons in our closet, something of which we should be ashamed. The truth of it is if your nightmares are truly skeletons, that's okay. Skeletons are old news—they are in the past, dealt with. The *demons*, the undealt with problems that are still alive and well, are killing you bit by bit. When you start shoving live demons into your closet before they turn into skeletons… Well, that's when you have a problem.

So don't give up. Don't give up the fight to heal just because you had a setback. Don't cash it all in, say, "Well, I tried. I'm still messed up, so who cares? I know I don't," and then go on your next emotional avoiding binge, whatever that may be. If you find yourself there, get back up! Get back up and keep fighting. The old adage "one day at a time" for alcoholics rings true here too. Keep thinking about the whys for which you are doing this. Matthew McConaughey said in his Oscar speech, "If the whys are strong enough, you can accomplish anything." The whys may vary just as the nightmares vary for everyone. Your why may be the desire to heal so you can be a better parent to your children. Or it may be as simple as being able to look at yourself in the mirror again without hating what is looking back at you. You may have several whys, or there may be only one. But remember why you are on this healing journey, and then get back up and keep putting one foot in front of the other forever!

Questions to Ask Yourself

1. What are the demons or skeletons in your closet?
2. What demon is festering in your life that you need to remove or heal from?
3. What scars can you identify that throw you into turmoil? How can you deal more positively with these triggers?
4. What unspoken words would you say to someone if you thought they would be gone tomorrow?
5. What are your whys on your journey through life?

CONCLUSION

Accept my past, love my present, stay by my side
because you want to be part of my future.
Everyone else, get out of my way!

This book is part of my journey to survive my past and succeed because of it. As dysfunctional as my actions were in the past, I know I dealt with things as best as I could at the time. This is what everyone is doing—dealing with what life throws at them with the tools and level of awareness they have in that moment. It is my mission to give people better tools to handle the big curveballs.

I wrote this book for all the parents out there. One thing that always terrified me was the idea I might pass my dysfunctions along to my children. In developing the concepts in this book, I always considered how I could teach my children to make healthier decisions than I did. In doing so I incorporated all the things my parents taught me—sometimes by emulating them and sometimes by taking a different tack. I always let my kids know, just as my parents let me know, that they are loved and cared for beyond imagination and that I will always be there for them. However I also encourage them to share with me even those things they are ashamed of or feel I will not agree with. In a fast-paced world where children grow up far too soon, this will be all the more important as they navigate their way into young adulthood. Like any parent all I can hope for is that I have prepared them for life, and I pray they make healthy choices.

I also wrote this book to help those who have endured a rape or other sexual abuse. It is difficult to explain to someone who has not walked that path how badly it breaks you inside. It breaks you physically, mentally, and—worst of all—spiritually. It does not matter whether it was a violent attack or whether the victim was blackmailed or otherwise coerced. He or she is left feeling like damaged goods—a terrible, soul-crushing feeling that lasts long after the physical wounds heal no matter how many people tell you it wasn't your fault.

In my case the attack, coupled with my strong religious upbringing, created a perfect storm of shame. The man who raped me not only violated my person, but he stole the one thing I thought should be safeguarded for my future husband. As a result I felt like I wasn't pure anymore and therefore unworthy of God's love. My mind chatter constantly affirmed this, telling me I was no longer wholesome and had nothing left to offer anyone—that was if anyone dared to love me at all. My entire being cried out for my lost innocence while my brain played and replayed the different choices I could have made. It did not matter that I was a victim; I always felt like there was something else or something more I should have done. *If only I had not gone to the party.... If only I hadn't gone in the room with him.... If only I had fought harder.* Those thoughts continued until that day, twenty years later, when I was finally able to forgive myself. Advocates may say I did not need to forgive myself—that I am wrong to blame the victim, even if the victim is me. This is all well and good, and in theory I agree with them. Nevertheless the fact of the matter is most victims, particularly young ones, will blame themselves if only because it gives them the illusion they were in control.

Rape victims fear what their friends, families, and spouses will think of them. Society's views on rape have changed since my attack, but they have not changed *that* significantly. Without the proper help and support, victims will still feel the shame and the need to prove themselves as worthy.

What they will find, again and again, is that we can never really change what others think of us. The truth, and ultimately the blessing, in all this is that we judge ourselves much more harshly than anyone else judges us. We hang the "damaged goods" sign around our own neck, and only we can take it off. When we do, we can heal our broken spirits and even recover that lost sense of wholesomeness. There is no such thing as a knight in shining armor. No one, not even the most well-intended spouse, parent, or friend can rescue us from our demons. To believe they can is just as unrealistic as believing in a fairytale. But you can—and must—be your own knight. You are the only thing that can save you!

On the other hand, how do you do this? How does one turn their nightmares around? The first step is to learn to accept them as part of your life; then you can begin to accept the pain in a useful way rather than trying to avoid it. For thirty years I bottled up my feelings because they were too painful for my heart to bear. However in forcing myself not to feel pain, I unfortunately lost some of my ability to feel positive emotions. I lost touch with love and how to love because every time I felt something good, it was immediately followed by overwhelming pain. Eventually, trying to avoid pain became a major focus in my life. Since thinking always led to painful things, I knew if I just kept myself busy enough, or if I just drank enough, I could turn off my mind and the pain along with it.

Through this process I have realized I am strong enough to face and conquer pain. And there are times when I have plenty of it. Pain from scars, pain from life—just like everyone else. The difference is the pain no longer has control over me, and when it does rear its ugly head, I know it will pass as long as I allow myself to feel. Music has been a powerful tool in this regard; it helps me bring up and cleanse pain and reminds me how far I've come. Now, when a certain song comes on the radio, or a picture or story from the past presents itself, I don't rush to turn the radio station or avoid an uncomfortable conversation. Instead I honor the emotions these things bring up; it means my heart is alive and well and capable of feeling. And that, after everything I've been through, is truly a miracle. Most important, it allows me to feel loved by others rather than simply knowing it in my mind.

Ultimately the real freedom has come in allowing people to see the real me instead of the perfect façade I constructed. The decision to do so came with writing this book, when I knew I would have to reveal things I had always kept secret. True freedom from nightmares means doing whatever is necessary, even if it comes at a great loss. We have to be willing to risk everything— even those people or things we feel we cannot live without—in order to heal.

My mother once said, "We are only as healthy as the secrets we keep" and with good reason. When we reveal things about ourselves, there is not always a happy ending—you may lose a friend or even a spouse. But as hard as this is, you will have gained something infinitely more valuable: your freedom. Freedom to be the person you were meant to be. Freedom to put down your burdens forever! Love yourself enough not to care about what people do with your secrets. Just rejoice they don't control you anymore. You can move on to live a more authentic, happier life.

Closure at Last

I had made so much progress since the events of that night twenty-two years ago. By focusing on the Five Fs, I had rediscovered what was most important in life, and many of the nightmares had faded into obscurity— more like that scar on my leg than the gaping wound in my heart. I was no longer the teenage victim but a grown woman who was married to the man of her dreams, with four beautiful children and a business of her very own. Most important, my perspective had shifted to one of gratitude. I was no longer someone who felt cursed; I *knew* myself to be someone who is truly blessed.

There was just one thing I still couldn't shake, and that was the lack of closure with my father. The horrible truck accident had robbed me not only of a most beloved parent but of the opportunity to come clean about the rape and see whether he could still love me.

No matter how many steps I took forward, no matter how many demons I slew, that one obstacle was always there, haunting me. Truthfully I never expected it to go away—it seemed as irrevocable as his death and something I would carry around until I joined him in heaven.

I got an idea one day from my friend, Drew, who seemed to have a fascination with the cemetery. He would often text me, "I am at your Dad's grave today." I would text back, "Tell him hi for me." To be honest he visited there much more than I did. So as this process came to a close, I knew what I had to do to finish it. I had to go to Dad's grave, to speak with him. I was ready to lay my burdens down once and for all, and because of this process I finally felt able and deserving of the chance to be free from them.

The day I chose for the visit was bright and beautiful. I drove back to Wausa with the radio turned up, allowing myself to get lost in music. When I got to town, I headed straight to Mom's house. I called to tell her what I was planning to do, and she was very supportive. She also knew how difficult it was for me, even after all this time; perhaps it was why she had never suggested it. For a while we sat together on the porch swing, me crying and her rocking me, just as she had when I was young. Finally it was time to go. I didn't know whether I was ready to face the grave site or not, but I had reached the point of no return. That's the thing about healing—in order to keep from sliding back, you must keep moving forward. I stood up from the swing, and after promising to call her later, I hugged Mom and headed back to my car.

A few minutes later, I was at the cemetery, passing row after row of immaculately kept graves. All these years later, and it was still surreal to visit my father there. My stomach was in knots as I turned down the row, walked up to the familiar black gravestone, and sat down cross-legged on the grass in front of it. We'd had the stone engraved with Dad's picture, and as always I was struck by the likeness; it somehow made it more real as I spoke to him. Of course I had never spoken to him like this before, and I stared at the picture for several minutes, just trying to gather my strength. I had rehearsed this conversation a million times in my mind—before and after his death—but now I was at a loss as to how to begin.

"Hi, Dad," I began tentatively. "It's Shandy…" And then I fell silent.

Suddenly I realized I had a lot of other things to tell my dad—good things that had happened since he had passed. Of my four children, he had met only my daughter, Shelby. She had been just eighteen months old when he'd died, but they had already laid the foundation of a lifelong bond. One day, as Dad worked on the electrical outlets in our house, little Shelby decided to "help" by dragging his tools away. He'd set something down only to find it gone when he reached for it again. It was so funny that Jason whipped out the video camera to record the scene. We'd thought we were taping an early video of our first child, never dreaming that we were making the *last* video of my father.

"Remember that day, Dad? How Shelby followed you around, watching your every move? We still smile when we think about it. Shelby is a teenager now, if you can believe it! She looks a lot like Wendy, with her long hair and gorgeous smile, and she is always trying to help her friends. She's a beautiful person inside and out. Oh, and she has your voice, Dad, and we all love to hear her sing.

"And then there's Logan—he was born two years after your accident. He's ten now, and oh, Dad, you two would have gotten along so well! He loves being outdoors, hunting and playing games. And even though he's never met you, it's like he feels this connection to you. He often looks at your pictures and asks about you. And I believe he's even seen your spirit. It happened the day I dropped off Shelby for her first full day of kindergarten. Like a lot of moms, I think it was more traumatic for me than it was for her, and as I saw her standing there on the playground, I was nearly in tears. Logan, who was only four at the time, looked up at me and said, in a very serious tone, 'Don't be sad, Mommy, Shelby is not alone.'

"I laughed and said, 'I know, honey, her teachers are there.'

"Logan shook his head. 'No, Mommy, that man was holding her hand.'

"Man! I whipped my head around to look back at Shelby. She was standing with the other children, and there was no man in sight. Still nervous, I stooped down until I was eye level with Logan.

"'What man, Logan?'

"'You know, the one from the pictures.'

"*Man from the pictures?* I had no idea what he was talking about. I asked him about the man several more times, but he just kept repeating the same thing. Finally I chalked it up to childish imaginings and headed for the car. But I was still thinking about it when we got back to the house. Once again, I bent down to Logan.

"'What man, Logan?'

"This time he did not answer me; he just went over to picture on the wall and pointed at you, Dad. Well, of course I burst into tears. It's one thing to hope and pray that our loved ones are still with us after they've passed, but to see evidence of it, to know that you are looking after my children, well, it was one of the most precious moments in my life.

"Then there are our two youngest, Mason and Greyson. Mason's seven now. He's an amazing kid—

tough and athletic yet so loving. He's always giving us hugs and special love notes, and he's just as happy helping me in the kitchen as he is running around on the playground. What I love most about him, though, is how he treats his sister and brothers. He always puts them first, like when he gets candy and sets aside some for them. He is such a gentle heart, and you would have been so proud of him.

"Greyson is just three years old, but I think of all my kids, he reminds me of you the most. He's handsome like you were, and no offense, Dad, but he sure has your stubborn streak! But what amazes me the most is how neat he is, just like you were. He is the only kid I know who can eat spaghetti and not get a spot on him. Also in your footsteps, he already loves to talk and is constantly telling me stories.

"You're probably wondering about Jason too. Well, he's the same wonderful guy you remember—even better. In fact he's become a lot like you. Sure, he can't fix much or tie a fish hook very well, but he can talk to just about anyone and make them feel at ease. And like you he understands the importance of family. I know he misses you every bit as much as the rest of us. You were always part of the package when he married me, and he felt cheated when we lost you. We all felt so terribly cheated."

I paused for a moment, wondering how I would deliver the next bit of news. Then again, considering how Logan claimed to have seen him standing next to Shelby that day, I had every reason to believe Dad already knew.

"Mom is doing well. She remarried a couple years after you passed; I think being alone day after day was just too much for her to bear. Her husband's name is Ralph, and although he's nothing like you, he's a good man. I won't get into how hard it was for all of us kids to accept him into the family, but let's just say it didn't happen overnight. It couldn't have been easy for him either, but he's really stepped up to the plate. He's good to Mom, and he's been a loving grandfather to the eleven grandkids in the family. He could never take your place, Dad, but I just want you to know that your family is being cared for."

I filled Dad in on my siblings' lives as well. "You would be so proud of Marty, Dad. He took over your farm and has really done well for himself. I know you will be surprised to hear this one, but Wendy got the courage to follow John's career path and move all the way to Pierre, South Dakota. They are all doing very well.

"I'm really sorry we sold the house, Dad. You know, after your accident we did a lot of other work to it, all along the lines of what you and I had talked about doing. We added a new bay window and put a privacy fence around the backyard. We remodeled that upstairs bedroom to make a suite for Shelby. It was good enough for a princess, and that was how she felt sleeping in there. And I wish you could see the garden, Dad. We replanted some asparagus I dug up from your garden at the farm, and I grew Grandma's strawberries—it was like you and Grandma were there with us! But if I had to choose my favorite thing about the house, it would have to that big whirlpool bathtub you and I put in together. It's not just the tub but the memory of you and me working side by side. Remember that day, Dad? Oh, how you were irritated at me for buying such a big tub. It was such a difficult job getting it into that room, but that feeling of accomplishment when it was done was well worth it. I've relived that memory so often."

My voice trailed off. I'd been there nearly an hour and hadn't come any closer to saying what I had really gone there to say. I reminded myself of the vow I'd made earlier—that I would not leave the cemetery until I had bared my soul to my father. I deserved the chance to purge myself.

"You know, Dad, there are also some things—some pretty bad things—that happened *before* you passed away. Back then I thought I'd have all the time in the world to tell you about them, but then one day you were just gone." I took a deep breath and forced myself to look into the eyes of the picture. "And ever since that day, some part of me has been left in limbo..."

For the next hour, I spoke nonstop, telling my father every detail of the night of the rape, from the way Joe made me feel special, pretty, and rebellious to how he'd held me down in that back room at the party. How the whole time I had been silently screaming for my daddy to save me. I told him how Tim had forced me to tell Mom and how Mom had convinced me it was better to keep the whole thing a secret. Then my downward spiral after that—the drinking, the wild partying when I went away to school. Once I started I couldn't stop. I even told him about the night I almost drove my SUV into the concrete barrier.

When I was finished, I again placed a hand on the gravestone. "That's it, Dad. That's everything. I just wanted to let you know how terribly I've missed you all these years and how I need to know whether you still love me."

I closed my eyes and prayed hard for a sign, but none came. I cried and lay down in the grass over his body and cried more. I prayed harder for Dad to hear me and that God would allow him to give me a sign that he still loved me. But all I heard was the sound of the chirping birds overhead.

I got the strength to pull myself off the ground, and I said, "Well, Drew's right. Only cold stones and cold bodies live here." Then I went back to the other side of the stone to tell Dad's picture good-bye. As I leaned in to hug the giant stone, the most miraculous thing happened. The sun was strong that day, and after baking in it all day, the black stone was *very* warm. I placed my face in the nook between the curve of the stone and the protruding cross, and there was warmth all over my face—it was as if I had just snuggled into Dad's shoulder. Suddenly I could feel his arms wrapping around my body and his warmth holding me close. I could *feel* his love wash over me. And in those moments I knew without a doubt that he loved me no matter what I had done or what had been done to me. I had gotten a hug from heaven.

When I was able to stop crying, I stepped back and said, "You were an amazing man, father, grandpa, and husband. Thanks for all you did for me as a child. I had a great foundation of love upon which I can build my own family. I have learned to live without you. It hasn't been easy! I would rather have had one more hug, see your smile one more time, or have the chance to say I love you one last time. I know now that you cherished family like I do, and you were proud of me like I am of my kids. I am you and you are me. Thanks for loving me!"

As I walked back to my car, I was both drained of strength and filled with gratitude. After all that time, to be truly known by my father and to know that his love for me was not bound by the circumstances or timing of the physical world was indeed a blessing. And then it struck me: I had been yearning for these things not only from the human father who had raised me but also from the Heavenly Father, who of course is also not limited by this earthly plane. He had also shown me that his love for me is endless and unconditional no matter what had taken place in the past. I was his child, now and forever.

And in that moment, it was finished.

I no longer live with regrets about my life. Everything I've been through has led me to the wonderful life I have today. I wish I could go back in time, hug my younger self, and tell her, "It's OK to cry. It's OK to feel weak. It's OK to be sad. You don't have to be tough or a grownup yet!" But I can't, and so I tell *you*.

You are a special being despite your nightmares. Love yourself. There will never be another you. You don't get lost time back. Love yourself and make the most out of the moments you have right now! They are fleeting and go by quickly. Pass this message on to others. Together we will make a difference in this world, one person at a time."